SEA·KAYAKER'S
SAVVY
PADDLER

SEA·KAYAKER'S SAVVY *PADDLER*

More than 500 Tips for Better Kayaking

Doug Alderson

Foreword by Chris Cunningham

Ragged Mountain Press / McGraw-Hill

Camden, Maine • New York • Chicago • San Francisco
Lisbon • London • Madrid • Mexico City • Milan
New Delhi • San Juan • Seoul • Singapore • Sydney • Toronto

Ragged Mountain Press

A Division of The McGraw-Hill Companies

10 9 8 7 6 5 4 3 2 1

Copyright © 2001 Ragged Mountain Press

Library of Congress Cataloging-in-Publication Data
Alderson, Doug.
    Sea kayaker's savvy paddler : more than 500 tips for better kayaking / Doug Alderson.
        p.   cm.
    Includes index.
    ISBN 0-07-136203-7
    1. Sea kayaking. I. Title.

GV788.5.A43 2001
797.1´224—dc21   00-067336

Questions regarding the content of this book should be addressed to
Ragged Mountain Press
P.O. Box 220
Camden, ME 04843
www.raggedmountainpress.com

Questions regarding the ordering of this book should be addressed to
The McGraw-Hill Companies
Customer Service Department
P.O. Box 547
Blacklick, OH 43004
Retail customers: 1-800-262-4729
Bookstores: 1-800-722-4726

This book is printed on 70# Citation by R. R. Donnelley & Sons, Crawfordsville, IN
Design by Geri Davis, The Davis Group, Inc.
Production by Deborah Evans and Dan Kirchoff
Edited by Tom McCarthy, Alice Bennett, and Chris Cunningham
All photos courtesy Doug and Sylvia Alderson unless otherwise noted
Illustrations by Christopher Hoyt

CONTENTS

FOREWORD

It pains me to read this book.

Among the hundreds of inventive tips that Doug Alderson has collected here, many remind me of my own less-than-pleasant sea kayaking outings that prompted me to discover better ways to do things. Sitting in a cockpit full of cold water, losing an expensive spare paddle that was swept off my kayak's aft deck, pulling a PFD out of storage only to find that mildew had given it more black speckles than a brook trout—these are the kinds of experiences that motivated me to improve my gear, my paddling practices, or both. While many people know that necessity is the mother of invention, the worst of my kayaking experiences taught me that calamity is often its father.

Doing a reentry and roll in rough water eventually led me to Doug's tip number 100 on foot-operated pumps. Like many paddlers, I always carried a hand pump, but after I had rolled up, I was so busy bracing that I couldn't afford to take my hands off the paddle. I stared for a long time at the hand pump before finally conceding that without another pair of hands I couldn't pull it from under the deck rigging, let alone use it. After installing a foot pump I never had to think twice about getting water out of the cockpit.

It was only after a lot of suffering that I came to appreciate Doug's tip number 370 on foot care. "Wet and sweaty feet," Doug notes, "are prone to athlete's foot [and] trench foot." When I paddled from Québec to the Gulf of Mexico in the winter of 1983, my feet were constantly wet. By the last month of the trip my feet felt like they were on fire. At night I'd lie awake for hours waiting for exhaustion and sleep to bring some relief to the constant itching.

I can heartily endorse tip number 509 on creating a comprehensive, accurate checklist. When I packed for an evening paddle, I had such a mountain of gear in the van that it didn't seem possible I could have left anything behind. But when I reached the put-in, an hour's drive from home, I discovered I had no sprayskirt. (To tip number 99 advising the purchase of a spare sprayskirt I'd add tip 99(a): You can make an emergency sprayskirt by cutting a tight-fitting waist-hole in your cockpit cover.)

I wish this book had been available twenty years ago when I first took up sea kayaking. It would have helped me avoid having to learn many things the hard way. I think what Doug is offering in *Savvy Paddler* is a home-schooling course of sorts; you can get a great education here and become a savvy paddler without suffering through classes in the School of Hard Knocks.

Christopher Cunningham,
Editor, *Sea Kayaker* Magazine
www.seakayakermag.com

PREFACE

Deciding to travel by sea kayak and camp in a tent is an expression of the desire to do more with less, to simplify an otherwise harried existence, and to get closer to nature at least for a while. Yet simplicity isn't inconsistent with comfort, and to be truly comfortable we have to meet our needs not only for food, clothing, and shelter, but for adventure, entertainment, and safety.

The sea kayak is a marvelously seaworthy craft capable of venturing out when any other hand-powered craft would founder. Sea kayakers can propel themselves onto isolated beaches where the only route out is the one that got them in. This seaworthy mobility combined with load capacity makes a sea kayak unique. The sea kayak must be well equipped, carrying your food, clothing, shelter, safety supplies, and more. It's solid counsel that no amount of good gear or physical preparation can make up for a lack of skill or judgment. But it's also true that good gear and well-considered preparation can make a potentially slow, wet, and frustrating trip into a pleasure to be remembered fondly.

Like tipping a basketball already heading for the hoop, a tip here is a hopeful nudge, a subtle redirection. A good tip must be both effective and economical. Simply sticking some reflective tape on the bottom of a hull might save someone's life, and reused milk cartons should keep your cookies from crumbling.

You're invited to apply the offerings in this book to traveling along the shore in any craft small enough for one or two paddlers. The water need not be salty, and a double-bladed paddle can be exchanged for a single-bladed one. The best use of the information is to enhance the joys of paddling and spending time outdoors. I hope you'll find some ideas in these pages that will add to your sea kayaking pleasure and safety.

ACKNOWLEDGMENTS

Tips in this book have come to me from friends with whom I've paddled hundreds of miles and from other paddlers I've met only briefly. I've cornered a few people and pumped them for their best tips. I've gleaned tips by casually watching someone set up a tent or pack a kayak. Some have come from studying kayaks resting on the beach, though I never knew their owners and builders. Aboard ship, traveling to remote coastal launch sites, I've asked fellow adventurers if they had any good advice to pass on. To all the paddlers, sailors, divers, hikers, and boatbuilders who have given of their experience and wisdom, my sincere thanks for your good nature, patience, and sharing spirit.

Some ideas have come to me from other creatures. One large male wolf taught me to sleep with my camera in my tent. Visits from several black bears showed me where to place my tent so as not to intrude on their morning forays. My apologies to baby sea otters and harbor seals whose mothers dunked them in the cold water when I came too close.

The days of playing and the weeks of touring could not have happened without the good-natured support and encouragement of my wife, Sylvia. Calmly answering the radiotelephone during storm warnings, relaying messages about delayed returns, and driving into the night to pick us up when everything else had gone wrong, she is unique—patient and understanding beyond my ability to comprehend.

CHAPTER 1

LEARNING TO PADDLE A SEA KAYAK

*S*everal things can help make you comfortable and confident in a

sea kayak. When you look across the water at an experienced friend

or your instructor, the kayak, the paddle, and the paddler seem

fused into one graceful unit. It takes time to become one with the paddle, but you

can do a few things to aid in your progress and feel good while you're learning.

Beyond the shelter of the beach, a sea kayak must be a self-contained unit,

complete with systems for navigation, control, propulsion, and communication

and piloted by a competent skipper.

Learning to travel safely and efficiently in a sea kayak is best done with the help of a qualified instructor. The American Canoe Association, the Canadian Recreational Canoe and Kayak Association, and the British Canoe Union are examples of national paddling associations established by paddlers to meet the needs of paddlers. One of the primary mandates of these associations is education. State and provincial groups provide regional emphasis and often are aligned with a national association, offering instructional standards in line with the national program. In particular, the training of instructors is guided by published program outlines. Taking a kayaking course from an established business or club with instructors qualified under a recognized association will enhance your enjoyment and safety.

1 A week of competent instruction is worth a year of just paddling around.

2 Take a course through a local business, and ask whether a recognized national paddle sports association certifies their instructors.

3 Take a guided trip. If you're more interested in sightseeing and going places than in technical paddling skills, taking a guided trip will be a good introduction. Look for a trip that includes equipment and basic instruction focused on getting where you want to go. A few hundred dollars invested in trying things out may well save you a lot more in the long run.

4 Join a club. Clubs by their nature are good sources of information and support. Ask if the club is a member of a state or provincial paddle sports association. Many clubs offer accredited courses in sea kayaking and other instructional activities. Participating in club-supervised day trips and overnight excursions is an excellent way to meet other paddlers.

5 Read books and magazines and watch some instructional videos. Reading about kayaking is no replacement for qualified instruction, but having a good background will help. There's a great deal of good literature available once you know how to find it. Check with retailers and local clubs.

6 Get out and practice your strokes and rescues at the beginning and end of the paddling season. When conditions

This student is learning to roll in the mouth of the Coppermine River, Nunavut, Canada.

are perfect for paddling you'll likely want to do just that—paddle all day and keep things dry. Early spring is a good time for short practice sessions to hone your skills.

7 Set a goal for this year's skill development: greater edge control, learning to scull for support, or developing your "offside" high brace.

8 Learn to roll. The best way to be safe is to be a skillful paddler.

9 The best way to learn to stay dry is to get wet, often.

10 Take a wilderness first-aid course. Even day trips can take you to locations where emergency medical treatment is hours away.

Choosing a Course

Find out as much as you can about a course and the instructor before you pay the tuition. Word of mouth is always a good way, particularly if the information comes from several sources. If others have enjoyed a course and learned a lot from it, there's a good chance you'll be satisfied as well. There are several questions you should ask.

- Is the course offered under a recognized paddle sports association?
- How has the instructor been certified?
- Does the tuition include all equipment, including a boat, personal flotation device (PFD), wet suit, and paddling jacket?
- Does the course teach the skills you want to learn?
- Is instruction required before rent-ing equipment or taking more advanced courses and trips?
- Are there minimum requirements for enrollment in the course?
- Does the course include a final assessment of skills and knowledge?
- Does the course include pool time?
- What is the class size?
- Is makeup time or further coaching available after the course?
- What are the guidelines for the maximum wind and waves you'll encounter?

Pay attention to the questions the company or the instructor asks you. An experienced instructor will try to determine your level of experience and make sure the course guidelines meet your expectations.

Choosing a Tour Guide Company

Taking a guided trip can be a wonderful adventure. A great deal of your satisfaction will depend on how well the outfitter has matched the clients' skill and expectations with the demands of the trip. Once again, word of mouth is a good source of information. Trips of interest to beginners are often to the more popular destinations. You can probably find someone local who has taken a particular trip. Personal reports about longer, more distant adventures may not be as readily available, but in either case, collect as much information as possible.

- Talk to an experienced person who has gone on the same trip with the same company. Nothing beats direct experience.
- Paying a lot does not guarantee the best trip. Inexpensive and good is better than expensive and poor.
- Call the outfitters and ask about their experience. Do the guides have wilderness first-aid skills? Are they trained and certified through a recognized association?
- Can you talk directly to the guide who will be taking you out?
- Choose a company that has been in business at least two years.
- Avoid arranging trips through a broker. Talk directly to the company manager or guide who assigns the destination and the staff.
- Look for a company that returns your calls promptly. It should be easy to reach.

- The company should provide lots of pretrip information well in advance of your departure date. Find out about the general character of the trip. Is the emphasis on beach ecology, natural and human history, or the technical skills of paddling through tidal currents?
- Expect to pay a substantial deposit. It's to your benefit; outfitters who have to fill up a trip at the last minute are more likely to bring along paddlers without the right experience. Did they confirm receipt of your deposit?
- What's the cancellation policy? What would make the company cancel the trip?
- What's the client-guide ratio? What's the total size of the group?
- Will the trip be conducted under any special permits or land use regulations?
- What food services are provided? Does the guide cook three meals a day, or is the cooking shared among the clients? Can the outfitters meet your dietary needs?
- Listen to the questions the outfitters ask you. A good guiding company will want to assess you and will need to know your skill level and your expectations. You can learn as much about the company by listening as by asking.
- Do the outfitters provide introductory instruction? Will they teach

you how to look after yourself? Tell them about your skill and experience level.

- How far are you expected to paddle each day?
- Does the trip include hiking, wildlife interpretation, and history of the local area?

- Do you have to share a tent?
- Do they provide kayaks? Are double kayaks mandatory?
- Do you need your own PFD? Can you bring your own equipment?
- Do they have a pickup boat in case of injury or bad weather?

Beyond the Basics

Once you're comfortable going out for a daylong paddle in a sheltered location, it's inevitable that the sense of adventure will stimulate you to paddle farther and longer. It's wise to gain the skills necessary to paddle in conditions rougher than you'd normally choose to go out in. Sooner or later, regardless of how carefully you monitor the weather, you'll get caught in unexpectedly demanding sea conditions.

11 Gain some experience with moving water. Learning to paddle in moving water, which includes surf and tidal currents, will be a challenge, and it will get your attention. Any kayak course that involves moving water or surf will include sessions on how to roll a kayak. You'll have all sorts of wet fun learning new maneuvers and terms like broaching, maytagged, pearling, and bombproof and combat rolls (see the glossary for explanations). It's best to do this in safe, supervised conditions rather than trying it out unexpectedly.

12 Try paddling a short whitewater play kayak in some waves and current. You'll get the opportunity to try the various paddle strokes—edging, bracing, and rolling techniques—sometimes all in quick succession!

13 When you buy your own kayak, outfit the cockpit with foam thigh and hip pads so it fits your body (see photo, page 6, and chapter 3). You'll need to look at how other paddlers have outfitted their cockpits. Different bodies and boats require different approaches to making the cockpit fit. Excess space around your body in the cockpit will hamper your ability to control and maneuver the kayak. The best-fitting kayak is the one that is snug yet comfortable without being confining. When you're seated in the cockpit, your buttocks, lower back, hips, knees, and feet should touch the kayak. You must be able to enter and exit the cockpit smoothly.

Learning to Roll

Rolling is one more playful thing to do in your kayak. Once you can roll you'll do it just for the fun of it. Rolling a sea kayak is easy, but learning how takes some time and persistence. Many people paddle for years before they learn; others can roll before they can paddle efficiently. The best way to learn is to take lessons from an experienced instructor. Different kayaks, paddles, and body types require slightly different approaches.

One thing is certain: when you learn to roll your kayak your other paddling skills will improve as well, particularly your bracing. And if you have strong bracing skills, you're much less likely to need to roll.

14 You'll feel bravest and most confident when you're most comfortable. Before getting into the kayak, jump into the water and swim around a bit. Do some front and back somersaults. Float on the surface and roll like a log. Then sit in the kayak and, with the help of a coach (friend or instructor), wiggle around trying some twisting and tilting. With the kayak in the water you'll find you have a great deal more tiltability and discover that the boat is more stable and forgiving than you expected.

15 Practice "hanging out" in your kayak. If capsizing makes you anxious, you're probably quite normal. If you find capsizing your kayak and then sitting head downward disorienting, you're definitely normal. It takes time and practice to feel secure upside down in the water. Wear a diving mask and watch the fish as you hang upside down. Watch someone else roll. Learning to roll has a large psychological component; when you're relaxed upside down in your kayak, you'll feel very relaxed right side up. Once you're not afraid of capsizing, your other paddling skills will develop much faster.

16 Be persistent; once you can roll you'll wonder what the problem was. The more you practice, the better you'll get; repetition is an essential part of learning to roll, and holding your breath, like other skills, gets easier with practice. Remember to develop your rolling skills on both sides.

17 If you're physically comfortable you'll practice more. Buy a warm, dry paddling top. Use a nose clip or diving mask to keep water out of your nose and eyes. Wear a neoprene cap so cold water in your ears doesn't make you dizzy. But make sure you end your practice session by doing a couple of rolls without the comfort aids so you don't become dependent on them.

18 Don't overthink it. Rolling is one skill where the phrase "just do it"

thigh pads

hip pads

Current Designs

Hip and thigh padding.

A small, rigid paddle float helps when practicing rolling.

applies. Have a coach lead you through it. Rolling must be learned physically; you'll have to feel it to understand it.

19 Try a roll using a rigid paddle float, which keeps the paddle on the surface and lets you feel where it should be. Unlike an inflatable float, the flat face of a foam float will plane along the surface. You can make an inexpensive rigid paddle float (see pages 52–53). As you become successful, cut the float down to a smaller size. As you get better, continue cutting it down until it's insignificantly small.

20 If after a period of success you find you can't roll any more, go back to whatever aids you were using previously. Complete a couple of successful rolls and then return to practice without the aids. It's common to lose the ability to roll for a while; go get it right again, and the skill will come back more reliably than before.

21 Every time you go out for a day paddle, spend the last twenty minutes doing a few practice rolls. Remember, be persistent! There's hot soup and a dry towel on the beach.

22 If the water is too cold for comfort, you have all the more reason to learn to roll. Staying warm and mostly dry before and after a capsize should be a motivating force. Bailing out of a kayak is easy, but reentering in rough water can be very difficult and time consuming.

Putting Your Roll to Work

To roll a kayak effectively and reliably, both your body and your mind have to be trained. For most of us, our first impulse when we're unexpectedly tumbled by a breaking wave is to escape the cockpit and do a wet exit. This anxious reaction needs to be supplanted by a disciplined response to roll. Physical practice in rolling is the first step; learning to calm yourself and feel confident when everything around you is out of control is the second.

23 Convince yourself that you can roll a kayak. Self-talk is a recognized mental training technique for learning skills, correcting errors, increasing focus, and building confidence. Self-talk must be purposeful and positive, focused on success. Concentrate on what you want to happen and avoid thinking about what might go wrong. All this can take significant effort and must be practiced just as diligently as the physical skills of setup, sweep, and hip flick. Failed rolls will happen and must be taken in stride. You'll need to maintain your focus so you can complete a second attempt.

24 Picture yourself rolling successfully. Positive mental imagery is a powerful tool for building confidence and improving performance.

25 Visualize yourself in the conditions that make you feel anxious and stressed, and carry the image through to a relaxed and successful outcome. Create a clear visual picture of a roll that brings you upright and under way with grace and style, and replay it frequently.

26 Practice making a second or third attempt at rolling before you actually roll upright. After a purposely unsuccessful attempt, recapsize and while inverted establish the correct setup position you started with, keeping calm. By repeating the same setup you'll do a half roll and come up on the same side as the capsize.

27 If your roll on one side is weak, follow an unsuccessful roll on your weak side with a successful roll on your good side. You'll learn that one good attempt leads to a more successful second attempt.

28 Practice changing sides. After a failed first attempt it may be easier to set up for a second complete roll in the other direction. The momentum of a full roll is an advantage. Also consider that the first failure may have been caused by the contrary effects of current, wind, or breaking waves. Determining a preferred direction as you're executing a strong second roll requires a particularly clear head.

29 When you don't roll up quite all the way, sculling for support can get you a breath or finish an incomplete roll. Failed rolls are usually more than 50 percent successful; you reach the surface in an unstable position, then recapsize. Rather than submerging to set up for another roll, scull for support and execute a high brace. As a follow-up to a partially successful roll, this technique lets you grab some air, though taking a breath while still unstable can be risky. A positive mental image will keep you from panicked gasping the moment your face feels the air, and a cool head may let you get a controlled breath when the chance comes.

30 Practice rolling a fully loaded kayak, which can be easier than rolling an empty one. A heavily loaded kayak rotates much slower than a empty, light one. Take your time and give a loaded kayak time to capsize completely before you execute your sweep and roll.

31 In a loaded kayak, practice a half roll. The heavy load in the bottom can add enough stability that the kayak may not want to roll completely over. Practice capsizing and setting up on the "high" side, rolling up on the same side as the capsize.

CHAPTER 2

MAJOR EQUIPMENT PURCHASES

B uying a sea kayak and all the additional gear is a significant expense. If you're to get the best value for your dollar, purchases need to be well thought out. Once you have a kayak, you still need a sprayskirt, paddle, flares, personal flotation device, bilge pump, and paddling jacket. For most sea kayakers that's just the beginning. A tent, stove, tarp, sleeping bag, and sleeping pad head the list of camping paraphernalia. Browsing the gear stores and catalogs can pass the time during the off season.

Choosing a Sea Kayak

Accept the fact that no one kayak can be fast, stable, hold a straight course, turn effortlessly, pack easily, have bone-dry compartments, and also be lightweight, durable, and inexpensive. Furthermore, assessing a kayak's performance characteristics is more an art than a science. Think ahead to how you'll most often use the kayak. Will it be for summer day paddles across the lake photographing the ducks, weekend camping trips during good-weather months, or long-distance wilderness adventure at any time of year? Do you plan on fishing, touring, or performance paddling in waves and wind? There's no doubt that aesthetics plays an important role in choosing a kayak. Look for design features that serve a purpose and are well thought out, but if you really don't like the look of a kayak, it's probably not the boat for you.

32 Write down what you want to do. You can purchase a kayak that will meet one or two requirements very well, but the more performance characteristics you demand, the more compromises you'll have to accept.

33 If a particular kayak design claims to do everything well, more likely it does nothing well.

34 Take a variety of kayaks out for a "test drive." Ask if the retailer will apply the cost of some rentals toward the price of a new kayak.

35 Test a kayak on a windy day. A kayak's tendency to weathercock will be evident only with a fresh breeze (fifteen knots). With rudder or skeg up, paddle a straight line across the wind. Be aware of how easy or hard it is to keep the kayak on course.

36 Test paddle a loaded kayak. Feel and performance will be very different with a load on board. Try paddling the kayak with a cargo load of at least fifty pounds. You can use two-liter soda bottles filled with water as temporary cargo; snug them securely into storage areas near the cockpit.

37 Choose a cockpit size that physically fits you. You can and should do custom-fitting to the cockpit, but the kayak should feel good to start with. Your hips, knees, and thighs should comfortably touch the interior walls. Foot braces should be both firm and easy to adjust.

38 Kayaks without bulkheads and watertight hatches must be fitted with flotation bags—sturdy nylon bags that can be inflated by mouth. The bags are designed to approximate the interior shape of the kayak. When put in place and inflated, flotation bags will keep a flooded kayak afloat.

39 Look closely at the positions of the bulkheads and how they are installed. Bulkheads need to be durable enough to withstand the intrusive forces of a heavy load and, when the paddler has gone for a swim, the force of breaking waves entering the cockpit.

40 Consider having bulkheads custom-installed as close to the paddler as possible. This considerably reduces the volume of the cockpit so less water is taken on board if the cockpit floods, increasing stability. Also, the water can be pumped out more quickly. Moving the bulkheads will also improve the reserve buoyancy of the forward and aft watertight compartments and increase dry stowage space. Some paddlers put their feet on the forward bulkhead.

41 Check the integrity of the watertight hatches. If your test paddle does not include a few waves breaking over the hatch covers, pour a couple of buckets of water across the deck and look for leaks.

42 A day hatch within reach behind the cockpit is very convenient for holding lunch, extra clothing, and other items you may want while at sea. This compartment takes on only a moderate amount of water if flooded and does not compromise the stability of your kayak too much.

43 Ask experienced kayakers why they like their kayaks. Ask whether the hatches leak. Does the rudder jam, or does the boat have a strong tendency to weathercock?

44 Reach inside the hatches and feel for rough edges or sharp screw ends. Determine how much space is available. Bring along your sleeping bag and see how well it fits into different kayaks.

45 See if the seat position is adjustable. The seat should be as low as possible, but some seats can be adjusted forward and back. This can help in

End toggles. Use a bungee to stop a toggle from flapping in the wind during transport or dragging in the water. (See tip 49, page 13.)

deck line

⅛" bungee to restrain end toggle

END TOGGLES

Standing on shore, we watched a pair of paddlers sitting abeam in the wash from the incoming surf. The words "they better not stay there" were barely out of my mouth when one kayak capsized. The paddler, unable to roll up, exited and hung on to the kayak. The other paddled back and forth erratically. Shouting as I waded into the shore break, I couldn't get any response. The swimmer was obscured behind the capsized kayak, and the nearby paddler was not looking up. In a heads-up crawl, I made it out through the surf to find the swimmer had a dislocated shoulder but was unwilling to let go of the kayak.

I called out to shore for a kayak and towline, but none were to be had. Another kayaker paddled out to help. But their kayak, equipped with a rudder, had no end toggle to grasp. The handle, located ahead of the rudder, was of no use.

It took a considerable time in cold water to swim the paddler and the kayak to shore. A kayak with a stern toggle to safely grasp in the water would have been a great help and would have speeded up a difficult rescue.

trimming the kayak to distribute weight evenly and adjust for better performance.

46 Carefully lift the kayak onto your shoulder. It should be balanced for a safe and comfortable carry.

47 A rudder is effective at keeping a kayak on track, particularly moving downwind, when rockered hulls tend to wander off course, or across the wind, when the kayak tends to turn upwind. But rudders are mechanical systems that require maintenance and sometimes break down. Relying too much on the rudder when learning to paddle may make you too dependent on it for controlling the kayak.

48 Drop-down skegs controlled from in front of the cockpit are a simple and effective way to adjust the tracking of

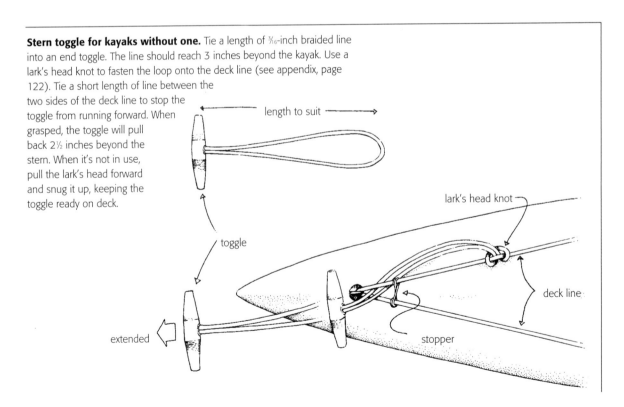

Stern toggle for kayaks without one. Tie a length of ⁵⁄₁₆-inch braided line into an end toggle. The line should reach 3 inches beyond the kayak. Use a lark's head knot to fasten the loop onto the deck line (see appendix, page 122). Tie a short length of line between the two sides of the deck line to stop the toggle from running forward. When grasped, the toggle will pull back 2½ inches beyond the stern. When it's not in use, pull the lark's head forward and snug it up, keeping the toggle ready on deck.

length to suit

lark's head knot

toggle

deck line

extended

stopper

the kayak, especially in windy conditions. When lowered, skegs counteract the effects of wind and waves pushing the kayak off course. Skeg boxes can interfere with packing the stern compartment, however, and the control cable must be securely fastened into the skeg box to avoid leaks.

49 Bow and stern toggles should be accessible to a swimmer's grasp. Toggles set in from the ends on the deck are meant for lifting the kayak and are not suitable for swimming rescues. Any toggle must be strong enough to lift at least a partially loaded kayak. (See illustration, page 11.)

Choosing a Paddle

You are the engine for your craft; your paddle is the drivetrain. You'll swing your paddle thousands of times each day. A few ounces less weight may not feel much lighter in the store, although the paddle costs $75 more, but the difference accumulates with each stroke.

50 Assess the durability of the paddle versus its weight. The lightest paddles, made of carbon fiber, are a dream to hold and swing; they're also the most expensive, but they can be brittle and may not stand up well to abuse around rocky shorelines. When traveling long distances through open water a very lightweight paddle is preferred. Paddles with fiberglass shafts and plastic blades are heavier but less expensive and stand up to the demands of paddling along rocky shores.

51 Two paddles of the same weight can have significantly different energy demands. A paddle with a heavy shaft and light blades will swing more easily

than one with a light shaft and heavy blades.

52 When comparing paddles, consider the shaft length and the blade length as separate measurements. The length of the shaft should permit easy paddling with the blade fully submerged. In choppy waves the paddle shaft must be long enough to reach down into the trough of the wave. Your choice of blade shape can significantly affect overall paddle length. A wider blade two inches shorter (with the same area as a longer, narrow blade) creates a paddle four inches shorter overall. This change in overall length will create a practical difference in the performance of the paddle.

53 Consider the blade length, width, and shape. Two paddles of the same area can perform very differently. A long, narrow blade has a softer feel and less immediate power. A shorter, wider blade will "sprint" through the tide race quicker but will feel less smooth on a long cruise.

54 A two-piece paddle is a little more expensive than a one-piece paddle, but it will fit in your kayak cockpit and your car trunk for storage and transportation. Two-piece paddles are plenty strong enough. If you're putting enough stress on your paddle to break it, it might break at the end, but seldom in the middle. Keep the coupling clean so it doesn't get stuck and you'll never have a problem.

55 You'll need a spare paddle for those demanding rough conditions when you lose or break your primary paddle. Budget your kayak purchase to leave enough cash for two good paddles. If you want to carry the spare paddle on the deck, it needs to be a two-piece model.

56 You could choose a paddle with a narrow blade as your primary one and a paddle with a wider blade as a spare or any other combination that suits your particular variety of paddling environments. Your spare paddle can be a different length than your primary paddle.

57 To choose a paddle length, start with an average of 90.5 inches for a lower (horizontal) paddling style and 86.5 inches for a higher (vertical) paddling style. Add or subtract 2 to 4 inches to account for a tall or short person, and add or subtract 2 to 4 inches to account for a wide or narrow kayak.

58 Round paddle shafts don't give any feeling for the orientation of the paddle and grip. A fingerboard or other index feature will do this. The fingerboard can be attached with heat-activated shrink-wrap or electrician's tape.

59 Take a paddle on a good long test drive, in a variety of conditions. It takes more than a few minutes to get the feel of a new paddle. The very short paddle may feel good sprinting in flat water or surf but be too short to reach the water in steep, choppy waves. The paddle is your only means of propulsion. Once you've done your research and confirmed your choice, buy a good one.

60 A paddle that's shorter overall will permit a greater variation in stroke rate. To navigate through surf or tidal rapids, you sometimes have to increase power and acceleration by stroking faster. For long-distance travel a slower, longer stroke is better.

61 Give both feathered and unfeathered paddling a good try. Nothing generates more controversy than asking two paddlers why one uses a feathered paddle and the other doesn't. Paddling aficionados and whitewater kayakers seem to prefer feathered blades. Tour-

Round paddle shaft with a fingerboard added. Fasten the fingerboard with heat-activated shrink-wrap, or simply tape it down with electrician's tape.

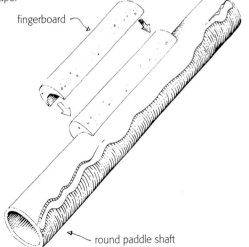

fingerboard

round paddle shaft

Paddle blades come in a wide variety of shapes.

ing sea kayakers tend toward lower angles of feather, and a great many use unfeathered paddles. Beginners seem to prefer the simplicity of unfeathered blades. An unfeathered paddle allows for identical left- and right-side skills. Paddles that are fully feathered (ninety degrees) require more demanding wrist and arm positions for offside maneuvers. A lower angle of feather will moderate the difference between control-side and offside techniques.

62 If you want to experiment or lend your paddle to a friend, changing the angle of feather on a two-piece paddle is easy. A few wraps of electrician's tape will keep the parts securely together.

63 To improve the grip on your paddle shaft, rub on a good quantity of beeswax or surfboard wax. A good grip is particularly important when kayak surfing or practicing rough water skills. For long-distance touring this not only will improve your grip but

may also avert blisters and calluses.

64 Make a paddle leash using 24 inches of ⅛-inch bungee cord. Fasten one end of the cord to the paddle shaft; the other end can go around your arm or be fastened to the deck using a loop, bead, Velcro strap, or small plastic clip. Make sure the cord has enough length and stretch so you can roll or do any other maneuver. It should give way if caught and not tie you to your kayak. (See photos below and top of page 16.)

−Adapted from *The Complete Book of Sea Kayaking*
by Derek C. Hutchinson

The paddle leash wraps on the paddle shaft when not in use.

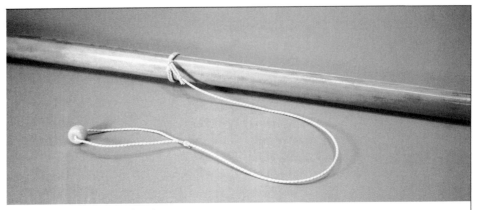

Paddle leash unwrapped and ready to use.

Personal Flotation Devices

You are required by law (in the U.S. and Canada) to have a coast guard–approved PFD on board. Approval indicates that the PFD is made of suitable materials with ample buoyancy and meets all coast guard requirements.

65 Buy a PFD that fits well and is comfortable, since this fundamental piece of safety equipment should be worn at all times. PFDs designed specifically for kayakers are shorter overall and have extra room at the shoulders and armpits to accommodate a full range of motion and unrestricted paddling. Look for adjustable straps and belts. The PFD you're willing to wear is always better than the one lashed to your back deck.

66 Test the fit. With the PFD zipped up and the straps adjusted, put your thumbs under the shoulders and lift up

PFD with large patch pockets and a whistle on a lanyard. The paddler is wearing a neoprene hood for warmth while practicing rolling.

A PFD with lots of shoulder room and adjustments assures a good fit.

TEST OUT EQUIPMENT AND MODIFICATIONS IN REAL CONDITIONS

A friend of mine spends a great deal of time during the winter adjusting and modifying his kayak and other gear. Always conscious of safety, he fitted a pouch pocket on the back of his PFD so he could always carry an inflatable paddle float. During a solo paddle in rough seas, he capsized and couldn't reenter his kayak. This was just the situation that called for his inflatable paddle float. But stiff from the cold water, he couldn't reach over his shoulder to open the pouch on his back. He had to remove his PFD to get the float, then he couldn't put his PFD back on properly because his hands were too cold to manage the zippers and buckles. With the aid of the paddle float, he reentered his kayak and tucked the PFD under the deck bungees. The self-rescue was successful but exposed him to greater risk.

firmly. The PFD should remain in place. A PFD that rides up around your face is too loose and needs adjusting or is the wrong size for you.

67 Toddlers and children must wear PFDs specifically designed for them. You must choose the right one. Put the PFD on the child and adjust it to fit, then pull up on the shoulders to simulate its natural buoyancy. If it does not fit properly, exchange it for one that does.

68 When buying a PFD consider your style of paddling. For long-distance touring, larger bellows pockets are very handy. More technical paddling may demand a PFD that will support a rescue belt and towline. Some PFDs accommodate a variety of accessories such as hydration systems, have places to attach a rescue knife and strobe light, and include an integral tow belt. Remember to keep it simple. Carrying too much gear on your PFD might weigh you down dangerously.

69 A pouch on the back of your PFD is another place to keep emergency supplies. If you're going to carry a separate pack, consider putting it on so the contents are accessible from the side. Attach short grablines to the items so access is easy and they remain secure.

70 Carefully consider whether attachments or alterations on a PFD will catch on anything. Avoid long lines; if items come loose they will tangle and be unsafe.

71 Make sure the straps of your PFD are fastened.

72 Look for a PFD that is highly visible. PFDs often come with reflective tape on the shoulders, or fabric sleeves with reflective tape attached can be slipped over them. More tape on the front and back would also be helpful, but be aware that attaching tape or other items directly to the PFD may invalidate coast guard approval.

Marine Electronics

Choosing to travel in a hand-propelled craft designed thousands of years ago while navigating with uplinks to multiple satellites may seem incongruous, but broadcasting a lifesaving Mayday call over a very high frequency (VHF) radio and simultaneously contacting the coast guard and a fishing vessel twenty minutes away is to some a highly desirable option. Using modern electronic devices can solve some problems and cause others. Electronics are expensive and prone to damage and malfunction. Radios, cell phones, and global positioning units (GPS) are well suited as backup to good traditional planning, judgment, and navigation skills.

73 Have at least one hard-shelled waterproof box. Durable plastic equipment boxes with O-ring seals are designed to hold radios, GPS devices, cameras, cell phones, or other sensitive and expensive equipment and protect it from getting knocked about.

74 Think carefully when deciding whether to keep your equipment securely tucked away or on deck ready for use. Kayaks designed with a day hatch accessible to the paddler are becoming more common. The day hatch can act as a large watertight equipment box. Radios, binoculars, and cameras are safe and dry while still within reach.

75 Remove batteries from all electrical and electronic equipment after each trip.

Very High Frequency (VHF) Radios

The handheld marine VHF radio can be considered a necessary piece of equipment. A VHF radio receives multiple continuous-broadcast marine weather channels. Channel 16 is used for marine distress calls and is monitored by the coast guard and most larger vessels. Radiotelephone calls can be made from handheld VHF radios to a regular land-based telephone service. Marine radios are also capable of ship-to-ship communications. Handheld VHF radios have a line-of-sight range of about ten miles.

76 Buy radios with large buttons and knobs. When your hands are cold, small buttons and especially small round knobs are hard to operate.

77 For easier operation, fit a larger ring onto a small on/off knob. Cut a

A day hatch is a good place to store items like radios and cameras.

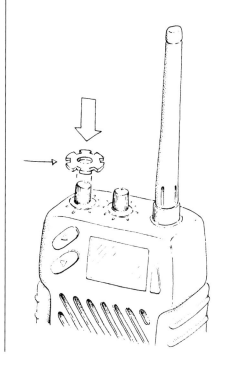

Notched on/off knob to help you use the radio with cold hands.

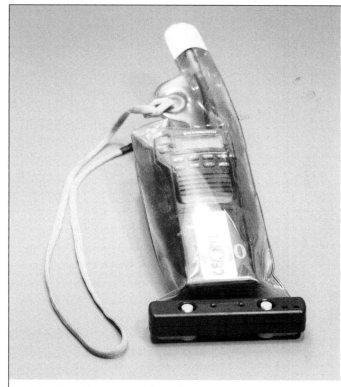

VHF radio inside a waterproof radio bag.

circle out of rigid plastic about a quarter inch thick, making the outside diameter as large as possible for your radio. Drill a center hole to fit tightly over the on/off knob. With the edge of a small file, cut a few square notches around the outside edge to give you a better grip. Press the notched ring over the on/off knob.

78 Cut an arrow out of reflective tape and position it to show clearly whether your radio is on or off.

79 Another option for protecting your expensive radio, cell phone, or GPS unit is a specially made waterproof bag. The device can be used while it remains in the bag, safe from the water. Air trapped in the bag may add enough buoyancy to make a radio float.

80 Inspect your waterproof radio bag regularly. Each time you recharge batteries, check for watertightness by squeezing it underwater in the sink. Watch for bubbles and leaks.

81 Open watertight bags at the first sign of condensation or other moisture. Very high humidity can develop inside and penetrate your expensive equipment.

82 Use your VHF while out at sea. A VHF radio is good for line-of-sight communications, so reception can be poor close to steep hills on shore. If you'll need to contact marine telephone operators or the coast guard, plan ahead; study the chart and choose a location where line-of-sight communications are not obscured by a nearby cliff or island.

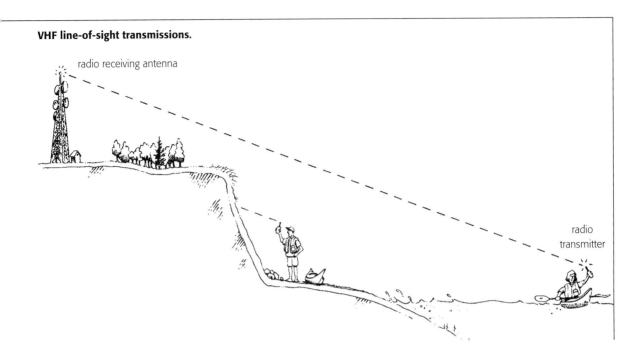

VHF line-of-sight transmissions.

radio receiving antenna

radio transmitter

83 If you don't have a VHF radio, you'll need a weather radio. Weather radios can receive several channels of marine weather broadcasts from NOAA (National Oceanic and Atmospheric Administration) in the United States and the Coast Guard in Canada. Buy a good-quality radio that will withstand the rigors of paddling and camping. The reception of some cheaper radios leaves much to be desired.

Cell Phones

With consideration for its limitations, a cellular telephone can be an excellent addition to your gear. Cell phone communication remains primarily a land-based technology; the marine search-and-rescue system in North America is designed to operate on VHF radio frequencies. As with any electronic device, the sea kayaking environment threatens reliability. A cell phone call only reaches one person, or perhaps a busy signal. A VHF radio broadcasts to all nearby vessels that have radios turned on. A cell phone can be a great help where reception is good but frustrating if not dangerous where reception is bad. When it comes to safety, don't rely on it as your only option.

84 When you call for a rescue with a cell phone, only one person may answer, or the number may be busy. When you call for a rescue with a VHF marine radio, you broadcast to anyone who is listening, including the coast guard and any nearby commercial vessels, which monitor the radio at all times.

Global Positioning Systems

On long passages across open water or along featureless shorelines a GPS unit can be a lifesaver. The technopaddler can't leave home without one. With satellites circling overhead, the kayak navigator need only press a button to fix an accurate position anywhere on the globe.

85 Make an extra battery pack. Two battery holders with four D cells each fit nicely into a plastic peanut butter jar. A wire extending through the lid with the hole sealed with marine caulking creates a tidy twelve-volt battery pack. I use one as an auxiliary battery for my VHF radio. Different-sized batteries in different configurations generate different voltages. Nickel-cadmium batteries put out slightly lower voltage than alkaline batteries, but ni-cads will deliver more current.

86 Waterproof electronics are waterproof only if you replace the stopper after recharging the batteries. Waterproof does not mean submersible, nor does it mean the device will float!

87 Do some research and shop for new models. In particular, GPS technology is changing rapidly. You can buy units combining a VHF radio and a GPS receiver, and some even include electronic compasses. You can also have your charts electronically loaded into the GPS unit.

88 Always back up your electronic systems with good standard navigation skills, a compass, and a marine chart.

Cameras

The path of the kayak leads to uncountable opportunities for graphic arts. Snapshots, photo albums, and holiday slides help you recount your adventures. Journals come to life with a few key photos.

89 If you store your good camera in a watertight, rigid box, keep at least a

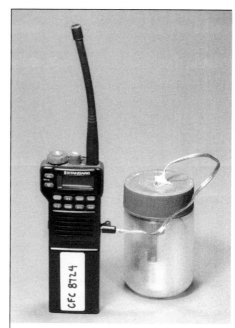

Supplementary battery pack.

cheap disposable waterproof camera accessible. Carry a camera as often as you can; some chances for a shot come only once.

90 Keep your waterproof camera out of the sand. One grain of sand under an O-ring can turn your camera into a teacup. Sand will also damage the telephoto mechanisms in water-resistant compact single-lens reflex cameras.

91 Plan photos. Action shots need to be set up. The normal motion of a kayak makes taking pictures of a moving subject difficult, and the focus often suffers. If possible, go ashore and use a telephoto lens to take pictures of friends paddling nearby.

92 Tell your paddling partners when you want to take wildlife pictures. They'll need to keep quiet and let you forge some distance ahead. Let them know how long you intend to paddle as a solo photographer.

THE UNEXPECTED

After a long day of paddling, I crawled into my tent. To catch the warm sea breeze I left the door open facing the beach. In the very early morning my eyes, opening to greet the day, met the gray-eyed gaze of a large male wolf. Thirty feet away he stood staring at me, framed in the outline of my tent door. I have the memory of that vivid image to live with always, but my camera was safely stored away in my kayak. Always go to bed with your camera in your tent.

93 Paddle backward when taking pictures. When you try to take pictures of shy and curious seals and otters they'll often follow close behind you, but as soon as you turn your head they dive and swim away. If you paddle backward they'll follow close in your wake. The faster you go the safer they feel and the closer they'll come.

Harbor seal pup at Race Rock Lighthouse, Vancouver Island, B.C.

CHAPTER 3

BEFORE YOU GO

*B*eing prepared is the best way to make your kayak expeditions

safe and enjoyable. This applies both to you and your kayak.

Outfit your kayak for comfort and safety, and make sure the

kayak's engine—your body—is fit and healthy.

A kayak, a paddle, and a PFD will get you started. Somehow, though, nothing is ever that simple. You'll also need a sprayskirt to keep water out and a bilge pump to get water out. You'll need a chart to show you the way and a compass to keep you going that way. Bungee cords, deck lines, and nylon straps hold down drinking bottles, charts, and spare paddles. Deck lines help you pull yourself back aboard, and towlines keep a hampered partner moving forward. After a time the cockpit that fit the beginner will need to be padded and adjusted to accommodate more advanced skills. When conditions outside are unsuitable for paddling, you can spend many hours installing new deck fittings or fussing over a new seatback. Outfitting a kayak is a never-ending process.

Sprayskirts

The sprayskirt is a humble piece of equipment, but its simplicity should not blind you to the demands placed on it. Without a properly fitting sprayskirt, the kayak is much less seaworthy.

94 A sprayskirt must fit the kayak. It has to stay on when waves break over the deck and when the kayak capsizes. Test the fit of a new sprayskirt by slapping it and pushing on it—it should stay on when pressed down firmly. But it should be easy to remove by using the release loop or pulling from the side.

95 A sprayskirt must also fit the paddler. Test the fit by putting it on over the type of clothing you'll wear when paddling. The tunnel should hug your body without being restricting. A snug-fitting neoprene tube will keep water out when you roll and be warm in cool climates. A loose-fitting nylon tube with suspenders to hold it up will permit the ventilation necessary to keep cool in hot environments.

96 Sprayskirts that have perimeter bungees prestretched and sewn into place generally fit better than those with the bungee cord pulled through a sewn hem and knotted on the outside. The knot in the bungee can interfere with the sprayskirt's snug fit on the coaming.

97 Make your release loop easy to grab. Loops made of nylon webbing tend to get folded under so they can't release the sprayskirt. Wrap electrical tape around the webbing to make a stiff loop that's easier to feel and less likely to fold under. Or attach a large plastic bead to the webbing.

Spray deck release loop wrapped with electrical tape.

98 Buy a cockpit cover. During transport or while you're sitting on the beach in a storm, it will keep out the rain. A kayak full of rainwater on a roof rack is likely to overstress the rack and possibly come off.

99 Buy a spare sprayskirt made of coated nylon. Nylon sprayskirts are less expensive, and they fold up small to pack away easily when touring.

Bilge Pumps

Every sea kayak must be equipped with a means of pumping water out of the cockpit. If the paddler is forced to remove the sprayskirt and exit the cockpit, a large amount of water will enter. If conditions are calm there are several methods for quickly removing most of the water and getting back in the kayak and under way, but if the sea is rough you'll need both hands to manage the paddle and maintain balance.

100 Foot-operated diaphragm pumps mounted on the forward bulkhead permit hands-free pumping. They're efficient and highly reliable. The forward bulkhead must be positioned to fit the paddler's leg length, and it must be strong enough to take the considerable stress of a strong leg pumping vigorously. Such a pump is usually considered a custom-fitted accessory. A foot pump can be expensive, but if you ever have to pump out your kayak in rough sea conditions, it will be worth it.

101 Diaphragm pumps are sometimes mounted on the foredeck. The pump handle is stored on deck and inserted into a fitting on the pump. This method of installation permits maximum punp efficiency but not hands-free operation.

102 A foot pump is out of sight and therefore can be out of mind. Like any mechanical equipment, it should be regularly inspected for wear and damage. Make sure the pump is clear of debris and that the one-way valves are working properly.

103 Carry a supplemental hand pump. When a hatch comes loose or a leak in the hull lets water into one of the storage compartments, you'll need a portable hand pump. Also, you and your paddling partner can pump out each other's boats.

104 Shorter hand pumps may be more reliable than longer ones. Longer pumps will pump more water per stroke, but when you're pumping furiously a long plunger is likely to get bent, rendering the pump unusable.

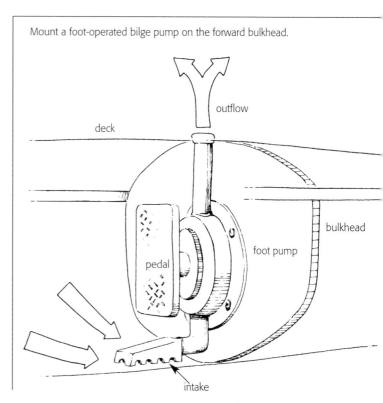

Mount a foot-operated bilge pump on the forward bulkhead.

outflow

deck

bulkhead

foot pump

pedal

intake

105 Electric pumps are efficient and free the paddler to deal with other concerns, but they require regular inspection and should not be used without a backup system. Batteries must be charged, and rechargeable batteries must be cycled regularly to ensure adequate power on demand. Properly installed and maintained, electric bilge pumps are ideal.

106 Make a strumbox (see illustration). A strumbox will improve the efficiency of your pump by minimizing turbulence at the inlet. It will also keep out some debris and may stop your pump from getting clogged.

107 Buy natural sponges or sponges designed for use in sailboat bilges. These sponges absorb many times more water than kitchen sponges. Keep one in the cockpit to absorb any water that is sloshing around.

Compasses

Marine compasses are different from compasses meant to be used on land. A marine compass has the bearing numbers printed on a plate that rotates to maintain its northerly orientation. It can be attached to the deck of a kayak without adjusting it. It's read by viewing the bearing as indicated at the lubber

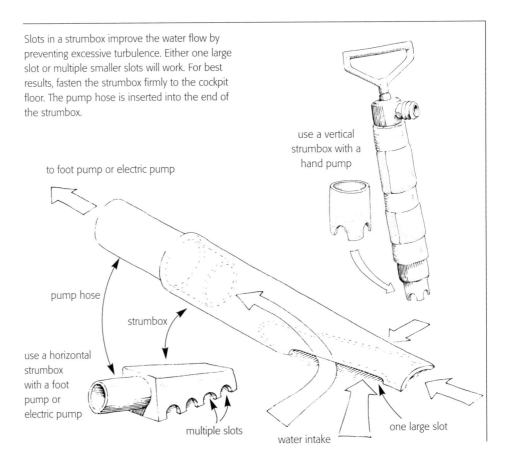

Slots in a strumbox improve the water flow by preventing excessive turbulence. Either one large slot or multiple smaller slots will work. For best results, fasten the strumbox firmly to the cockpit floor. The pump hose is inserted into the end of the strumbox.

use a vertical strumbox with a hand pump

to foot pump or electric pump

pump hose

strumbox

use a horizontal strumbox with a foot pump or electric pump

multiple slots

water intake

one large slot

line (a fixed line on the compass aligned with the boat's longitudinal axis). A marine hand-bearing compass, built the same but intended to be held in the hand, makes an excellent companion to a deck-mounted compass. (Puck-style hand-bearing compasses are well suited to kayak navigation.) Marine charts show the magnetic variation on the compass rose, so you can navigate using only magnetic directions.

In contrast, a hiker's compass has the bearing numbers printed on a bezel, and the backing plate is rotated to align the compass base with grid lines on a map. Hiker's compasses often permit a semipermanent setting to account for magnetic declination (a landsman's term). Compass bearings on land are in relation to true north, and the local deviation is added and subtracted accordingly.

It's best to work one way or the other. Mixing the two styles of compasses and navigation techniques is a sure way to get confused. Marine charts are designed to work with marine compasses and magnetic bearings. Land maps are designed to work with true bearings and map compasses.

108 Marine navigation can use magnetic bearings read directly from the compass rose on the chart. Bearings do not need to be translated to true north.

109 Buy a compass that will operate smoothly on the deck of a bouncy kayak. The quality of the compass movement will affect its response. Better compasses are liquid filled to slow their motion for easy reading.

110 Use heavy-duty Velcro to attach your compass mount to the foredeck. This product is very tough, and I have

Taking a bearing using a puck-style hand-bearing compass.

Deck-mounted marine compass.

Marine compass fastened to hatch cover with heavy-duty Velcro. The compass can be removed when not in use.

never seen a compass mounted with it come off in breaking seas or stiff surf. You can remove the compass for transport if you want.

111 Mount your deck compass well forward so you can read it while still looking ahead. The forward hatch is a good spot. Looking down while paddling in a rough sea makes some people seasick.

112 The Ritchie Sportabout compass is designed with an accessory holder that can be strapped to the deck. The compass can be deck mounted or used as a hand-bearing compass.

Deck Rigging and Layout

The layout of fittings, bungees, and lines is an important part of kayak design. Many paddlers will fuss endlessly trying to come up with the most effective arrangement of deck hardware. Deck lines, cleats, end toggles, control cables, and bungee cords help keep drink bottles, spare paddles, paddle floats, and compasses in place. A deck cluttered with too much paraphernalia or with equipment not securely fastened creates unneces-

The Ritchie Sportabout compass can be hand bearing (top) or, when in its tie-down holder, deck mounted (bottom). (Courtesy Ritchiesport)

sary hazards in rescue situations. In rough seas the last thing you want is lines dangling and equipment falling off.

113 Put perimeter deck lines on your kayak; they're considered a necessity by many experienced paddlers. Deck lines should be at least ¼-inch braided polyester, thick enough to hold on to comfortably.

114 Binding the ends of perimeter deck lines with spiral hitching (see illustration below and appendix, page 125) avoids lumpy and unsightly knots. Spiral hitching is more secure than other whipping techniques.

115 Thread large beads onto your bungees and deck lines or tie figure-eight knots at strategic spots to make it easier to slide your paddle or your fingers underneath.

116 Install bungees under your cockpit deck, duplicating deck fittings to take advantage of every usable space. To hold the bungees up you may also need to place some eyes on the top center of the cockpit. Make sure gear stored inside the cockpit doesn't interfere in any way with the paddler's exiting or reentering. (See illustration, page 30.)

117 To hold items in place and to help you slide them in, sew some vinyl-covered woven polyester netting between the bungees fore and aft to form a tray.

Wooden or plastic beads strung on deck lines or bungees make it easier to slide your fingers or a paddle underneath.

Binding the ends of two bungees or deck lines.

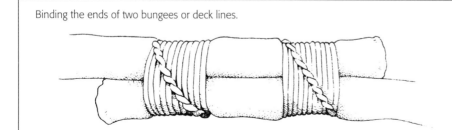

Underdeck bungees. Install these to match the bungees on top of the deck. A hand bilge pump can be stored conveniently under the deck. Plastic tubes can hold flares or a VHF radio. Folded charts or your pogies will store here close at hand and out of harm's way. Alternatively, a tray of neoprene or vinyl-coated polyester netting can be incorporated with the lines or bungees under the deck. Items stored in this way don't seem to interfere with entering or exiting the kayak, but check it carefully for yourself before you make any lasting additions to your kayak.

PVC tubes will keep your radio or flares safe and dry.

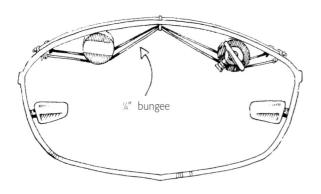

¼" bungee

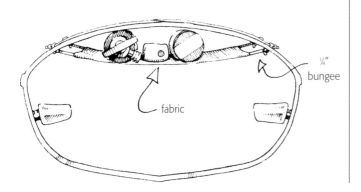

¼" bungee

fabric

Items placed on the netting are quite secure. (You can get the fabric from businesses that repair patio furniture.) **118** Fasten your sliding footrest rudder controls in the forward position. When they're pulled back, the control wire forms loops that interfere with reentry.

To prevent this hazard, attach a ³⁄₁₆-inch bungee cord from the footrest to the forward bulkhead using a small strap eye stuck to the bulkhead with caulking. This will create enough tension to keep the cable taut and the footrest in position.

119 Permanently tether your hatch covers to your kayak. Properly fitting hatch covers keep the water out and maintain the kayak's buoyancy, so a lost hatch cover is a significant safety risk. Some foam glued to the underside of the covers will keep them afloat if they do come loose.

Making Your Own Deck Fittings

Deck Line Fittings. You can make flush fittings to hold deck lines using domed end caps made for 1-inch white polyvinyl chloride (PVC) water pipe and the shafts of ⅛-inch to ³⁄₁₆-inch stainless steel pop rivets. Cut each end cap down to form half a sphere and drill holes on opposite sides to accept the pop rivet shaft. Separate the rivet from the shaft and push the shaft through the holes in the plastic cap. Use a hole saw to cut a hole in the deck the inside diameter of

Flush deck fittings you can make yourself.

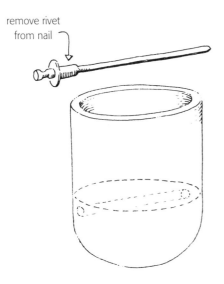

remove rivet from nail

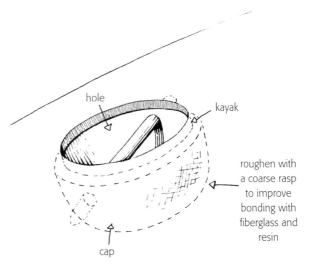

hole

kayak

roughen with a coarse rasp to improve bonding with fiberglass and resin

cap

the end cap, then use epoxy to glue the fitting into the hole, open end up. First thoroughly rough up the plastic with a coarse wood rasp and nick it in several places so the epoxy can lock in.

Strap Fittings. Use nylon webbing straps instead of bungee cords to store important items on deck, since they won't stretch when put under stress by waves. If you're a good do-it-yourselfer you can easily figure out a way to make fittings to hold the straps. (I had mine made by a school shop teacher.) (See photos and illustration, page 32.)

120 Use epoxy to glue some strap holders behind your seat and inside the cockpit area. Storage space in a kayak is at a premium, yet the cockpit often has an abundance of unused space. Gear stored there can be held fast with lines, straps, or bungees and will stay put without interfering with the paddler.

121 Keep your bow line short and out of the way. Long bow lines will hang down when the kayak capsizes and can catch the paddle when you're setting up for a roll. Attach the looped end of a short bow line to the deck line between the bow and the forwardmost deck fitting. Bring the other end back to the deck bungees. A figure-eight knot tied on

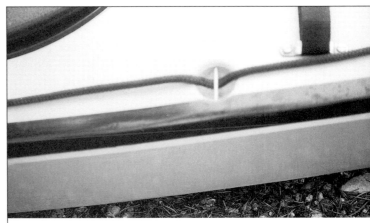

A do-it-yourself flush deck fitting installed on a plywood and epoxy kayak.

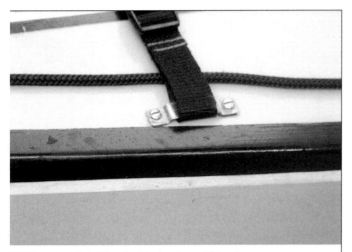

Stainless steel deck fitting for 1-inch nylon webbing straps.

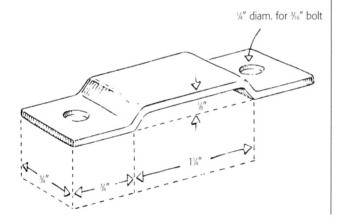

¼" diam. for ³⁄₁₆" bolt

⅛"

1¼"

¾"

¾"

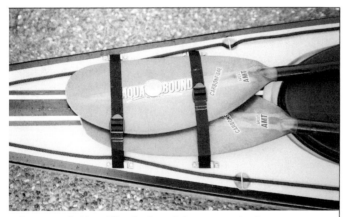

Nylon straps hold paddles firmly and do not stretch when waves come across the deck.

the end will jam under the bungees, keeping the bow line secure. When the bow line is used, the spliced end will run forward along the perimeter lines up to the bow. (See photos, page 33.)

Attaching a towline to your kayak is another of the many compromises kayakers continually struggle with. Mechanically, the best place to tow from is just behind the cockpit, but this location can be difficult for the paddler to reach. (See photos, page 34, and top illustration, page 35.)

Fitting into Your Kayak

As the motors for our human-powered craft, we need to be aware of our muscular force, performance, and efficiency. Before you try to build up your muscles by spending long hours in the gym, consider improving your performance and efficiency.

To sustain the effort of paddling for hours at a time, the paddler must fit securely into the cockpit. Comfort in a kayak should not be confused with spaciousness. Comfort can be improved by making the seat and cockpit support your buttocks, legs, and feet.

Power from your muscles is transmitted to the kayak through the lower body. When you travel forward, paddle power is transmitted through your buttocks and feet. For efficient turning, power must be redirected laterally to the hull by your hips and knees. Turning is more efficient when the paddler tilts the kayak on edge, and when you're paddling in breaking waves or currents, tilting improves stability. To edge the kayak effectively, you must have firm contact with the deck at the hips, thighs, and knees.

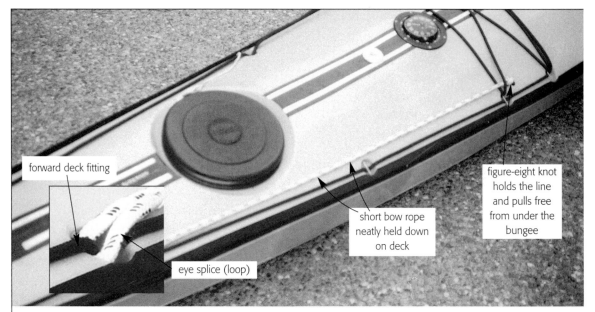

forward deck fitting

figure-eight knot holds the line and pulls free from under the bungee

short bow rope neatly held down on deck

eye splice (loop)

A short bow rope has one end snugged beneath deck bungees. The other end has an eye splice running along the deck line.

eye splice (loop)

The short deck line is pulled free of the deck bungee; the eye splice has run forward along the deck line.

122 Glue a thin neoprene pad onto your plastic bucket seat. It will stop you from slipping around, add some padding, and be much warmer. If you find there's a pressure point on your buttocks so that your foot or leg goes to sleep, glue a neoprene double doughnut on the seat. The holes in the doughnut should relieve the pressure on the nerves and bring your extremities back to life.

123 Use marine caulk to glue foam pads into your cockpit. It's much less sensitive than contact cement, so it's

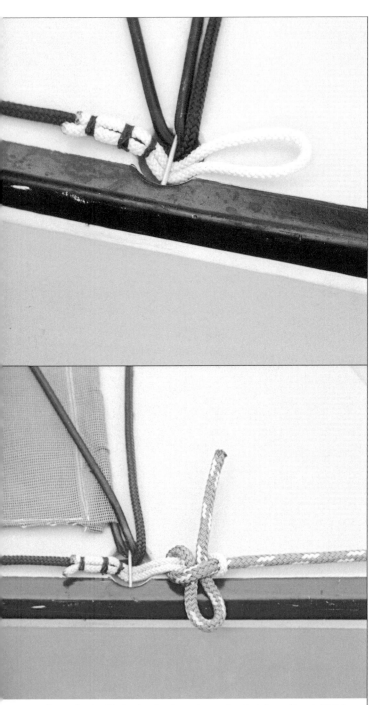

A loop of ³⁄₁₆ braided nylon line bound onto the deck line with spiral hitching (see appendix, page 125) is a good way to attach dock lines and towlines. (See text, page 32.) A quick-release sheet bend (see appendix, page 126) is another good method.

easy to apply, and it doesn't break down in the marine environment.

124 If more than one person uses your kayak and the foam padding doesn't fit both, use Velcro to fasten hip and knee pads to the inside of the cockpit. Pads of different sizes can be attached for each user.

125 To remove a stubborn sticky mess like old foam residue, use Goo Gone. It will instantly remove the toughest caulk and won't harm fiberglass surfaces.

126 Cut your foam with a hacksaw. Inexpensive one-handed hacksaw blade holders are particularly good for this purpose. An extended flexible hacksaw blade will cut a curve.

127 Glue a piece of neoprene or ¼-inch foam under your feet in the cockpit. It will keep your feet warmer and prevent sandy boots from wearing a hole in the hull.

128 Modify your seatback or install a backband (shown in the photo on page 35.) Tall seatbacks dig into the paddler's side or lower back, interfering with deep bracing and rolling. Tall seats also interfere with reentering the cockpit. The seatback should be lower than your cockpit coaming.

129 Drill a couple of ¼-inch holes in the bottom of your fiberglass bucket seat to let the water drain out. A roll of fine sandpaper pushed in and out and twirled around in the holes will round off the sharp edges and help prevent cracking. Seal the edges of the holes with a little five-minute epoxy.

130 Lower your seat. Many seats in ocean kayaks are raised up from the hull. Lowering the seat as little as half

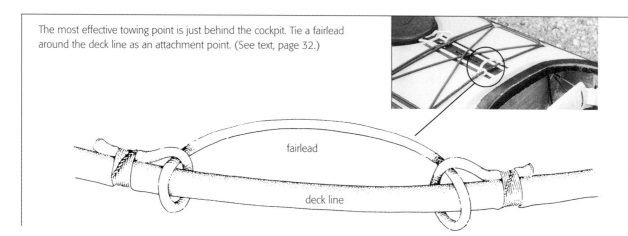

The most effective towing point is just behind the cockpit. Tie a fairlead around the deck line as an attachment point. (See text, page 32.)

fairlead

deck line

an inch can make a difference in stability. Removing a too-thick seat pad or sanding out a deeper contour in a foam seat can also lower the seat and increase stability.

131 You'll sit more comfortably if the bottom of your seat is an inch higher at the front than the back.

Tethers

132 Ropes and tethers attached to your body or the deck can be a significant hazard. Keep them well contained to avoid entanglement.

133 Never paddle in fast-moving water or breaking waves with anything tied around your neck.

134 Check that tethers and straps can be undone with cold hands. There's a

foam padding cut with hacksaw

backband

neoprene padding on seat

Cockpit modified for comfort and performance.

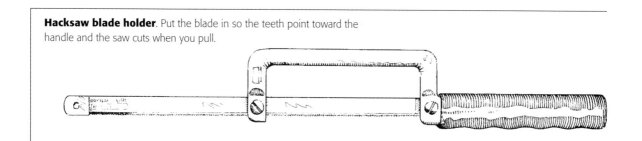

Hacksaw blade holder. Put the blade in so the teeth point toward the handle and the saw cuts when you pull.

DECK AWASH

I was preparing to leave a beach through low surf with only my chart and water flask on deck. The chart was in a large Ziploc bag firmly held flat by three stiff ¼-inch bungees stretched across the deck. The surf was quite small, and the spilling break was only 4 feet high. Timing my exit to coincide with a lull in the wave pattern, I paddled away from shore. As so often seems to happen, I mistimed my leaving and paddled straight out into the first wave of the next set of incoming breakers. The wave crashed into my chest and face, and its force pulled the paddle out of my left hand. To add to the confusion, the chart was now relocated where the wave had just passed, over my chest and face. Since I couldn't paddle or even see, it was quite a surprise that I didn't capsize and was able to sort out my predicament before the next wave.

delicate balance between having spare paddles and other safety gear well secured and being able to get them loose when you need them.

135 Use deck bungees with caution. Even modest waves will remove almost anything stuck under them. Equipment tied to a bungee cord with a line can come free and dangle around the cockpit. This is particularly hazardous during a capsize and can be very awkward during reentry.

136 Before landing or launching on a beach through surf, remove all gear from the deck.

Repair and Maintenance

Survey your kayak and make sure you have the necessary bits and pieces to repair or replace all fittings and mechanical parts. Keep these in a repair kit. Include nuts, bolts, cables, cable clamps, deck lines, deck fittings, bungee cords, buckles, straps, and the tools to install them.

137 Always test new equipment. A seat cushion may come loose and get jammed forward when you reenter the cockpit. You may not be able to open plastic buckles with cold hands.

138 Occasionally wash out the interior of your kayak. Food smells can accumulate that are unpleasant for you and attractive to animals. A dilute bleach solution will clean and deodorize your boat.

139 Plumber's waterproof grease is good for lubricating carabiners and folding knives. Use a toothpick to apply the right amount.

140 Vinegar removes hard-to-reach encrusted salt deposits. A couple of tablespoons of vinegar in a basin of warm water will help you get salt out of watches, waterproof cameras, folding knives, and other equipment.

141 Two-part epoxy putty available in a single-stick form is a good repair tool. It sets up in just a couple of minutes, even when wet. It dries rock hard and can be drilled, painted, or covered with fiberglass.

142 Tether your skeg. Drill a small hole in the lower end of the skeg, tie

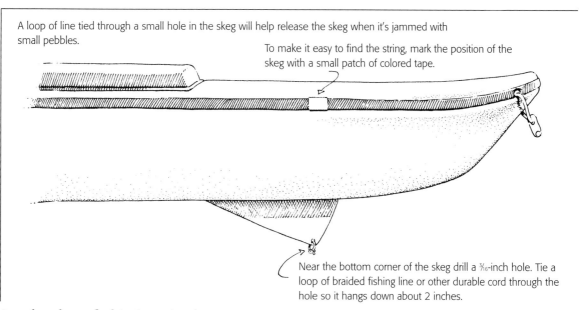

A loop of line tied through a small hole in the skeg will help release the skeg when it's jammed with small pebbles.

To make it easy to find the string, mark the position of the skeg with a small patch of colored tape.

Near the bottom corner of the skeg drill a ⁵⁄₁₆-inch hole. Tie a loop of braided fishing line or other durable cord through the hole so it hangs down about 2 inches.

in a short loop of whipping twine (see tip 158, page 39), and mark its location with tape on the sheer line along the hull. When the skeg is jammed, slide up alongside your paddling partner, who can then reach under your hull at the point marked on the sheer line, find the twine, and pull down on the loop. Replace the twine when it wears out or breaks.

143 Prevent the skeg from picking up pebbles. If you're on your own and can't have someone else clear the skeg, you need to avoid its getting jammed in the first place. Fold the end of a piece of tape over several times to make a padded end 1 inch long. Punch a small hole in the pad, thread some whipping twine through, and tie it onto the tape. Cut a piece of the tape long enough to cover the opening of the skeg box on the keel of your kayak. Put the tape over the opening with the folded end of the tape nearest the stern. Cut the piece of twine long enough to reach forward to the cockpit. Press the tape

COCKPIT CHECKLISTS

Glue a checklist with personal identification information on the inside of your cockpit. Many kayaks come with a simple checklist. If yours doesn't or if the checklist is too brief, fasten a plastic laminated list there and check it every time you go out.

This kayak belongs to: *Doug Alderson (555) 456-1234*
In case of emergency, contact: *Bob Brown (555) 345-6789*
VHF call sign: *VJ2591*

- ☐ **PFD**
- ☐ **wet suit**
- ☐ **drinks**
- ☐ **food**
- ☐ **towline**
- ☐ **hat**
- ☐ **paddling jacket**
- ☐ **paddle**
- ☐ **paddle float**
- ☐ **spare paddle**
- ☐ **flares**
- ☐ **VHF radio**
- ☐ **buoyant throw line**
- ☐ **change of clothes**
- ☐ **emergency shelter**
- ☐ **float plan filed**

down firmly and get ready to launch. The tape needs to stay on the keel only during the launching. Once you're off the beach and paddling you can pull on the twine to strip off the tape, leaving a clean, unjammed skeg.

Kayak Maintenance Checklist

Regular maintenance will keep your kayak shipshape. Remember that if your paddling partner has a maintenance problem, so do you. When you're speeding down the face of a 6-foot wind wave, you want all systems on your kayak in good working order. If the end of a rudder cable comes loose it will have significant consequences.

144 Look before you launch. At the beginning and end of each season, and before and after each long trip, thoroughly inspect your kayak for wear and damage.

145 Put your head in the hatch and use a mirror and a flashlight to check the ends of the kayak. You may be surprised at what you find.

146 Check bulkheads for leaks and cracks. Flexing can make bulkheads separate from the hull. Breaking waves entering the cockpit during rescue practice stress bulkheads. Paddlers who use the forward bulkhead as a footrest put heavy loads on bulkhead seams.

147 Check the seam between the hull and the deck. Waves striking the kayak from the side and paddlers lifting loaded boats are two common causes of deck/hull seams parting. Look for cracks and more obvious defects both inside and outside the hull.

148 Check the joint between the cockpit coaming and the hull. Using rescue

stirrups and lifting the kayak by the coaming put heavy stress on this seam.

149 Check both inside and outside for deep scratches in the gel coat. Barnacles scrape deep into the layers of cloth, and water will infiltrate the frayed glass fibers and increase the damage. Sandy heels and loose seats rubbing on cockpit floors have worn clear through some hulls. Keels have worn through and caused leaks in watertight stern compartments. Have all deep scratches and worn spots repaired.

150 Check for loose or corroded metal deck fittings and fasteners. Replace any fittings that might fail in the next year, bedding the new fittings in good-quality marine sealant or caulk.

151 Check rudders and skegs, particularly where different metals are joined, such as where aluminum footrests meet stainless steel cables and fasteners. Rudder or skeg control cables with shredded strands need to be replaced. Look for bent rudders and skegs. Rudders must operate smoothly; check that they will turn fully left and right without jamming.

152 Chafed deck lines should be replaced. Pay particular attention to lines that attach bow, stern, and carrying toggles.

153 Check that foam padding is firmly glued in place. Hip, thigh, and knee braces that have come loose need to be replaced or reglued. You may want to improve the fit by installing new padding or adding more.

154 Inflate flotation bags and carefully check for leaks.

155 Wash off your kayak with lots of clean fresh water after each use and

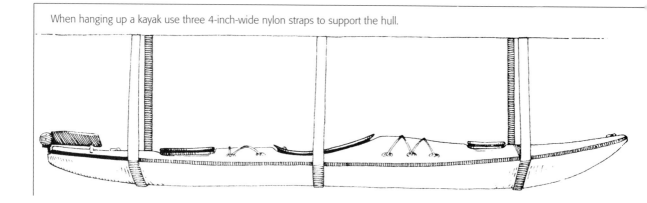

When hanging up a kayak use three 4-inch-wide nylon straps to support the hull.

store it under cover. Fiberglass and plastic deteriorate when exposed to salt and sunlight.

156 If you hang up your kayak, support its weight with three 4-inch-wide nylon webbing slings spaced evenly along its length. Plastic can deform under small stresses if given enough time, so bulkheads and deck seams may begin to leak.

157 Loosen the hatch covers for storage. If they create an airtight seal, variations in temperature will make the kayak and the covers expand and contract, causing unnecessary stress and wear.

Hardware

"A place for everything and everything in its place" is a phrase any boater is familiar with. One problem in kayak camping is that you need a host of small items and have no cabinet drawers to keep them in. Many bits of hardware lend themselves to being stored in fabric dry bags. One large plastic peanut butter jar will keep these items under control and within reach (see photo, page 40):

    whipping twine
    candles
    razor knife

    spare batteries
    nuts, bolts, screws, cable crimps
    lighter
    matches
    fire starters
    electrician's tape
    duct tape, masking tape, or packing tape; wrap it around the outside for easy access

158 Whipping twine, available at any yacht chandlery, is heavy waxed polyester that doesn't stretch and is light, strong, and rot resistant. It comes in small, flat spools; put one in your hardware kit. It's superb for binding deck lines, bungee cords, or any other job requiring a sturdy structural line. Use whipping twine for emergency fishing lines, repairing seams in sprayskirts or wet suits, making driftwood mobiles, and many other purposes around camp and kayak.

159 Dental floss works where you need to do finer stitching and repair.

160 Clear plastic packing tape is very tough and competes with the universal duct tape. Packing tape is smoother and flatter, and it doesn't weather as quickly or leave the gummy residue that duct tape does.

A large plastic peanut butter jar makes an excellent container for hardware.

161 In your emergency repair kit keep a piece of ⅛-inch plywood large enough to cover a hatch. Covered with a heavy plastic bag, the plywood makes a fairly robust hatch cover replacement. Fasten the plastic to the hatch coaming with a couple of wraps of ³⁄₁₆-inch line. The plywood can also be used for hull repair.

Health and Fitness

Kayaking requires a good level of overall fitness. A kayak's engine is the paddler's body, which can't be sent to the mechanic for rebuilding. New parts are very expensive and never work as well as the original equipment.

General Fitness

One of the best ways to get in shape is just to go kayaking—a lot. Include all the bending, stretching, and reaching involved in exits and reentries, rolls, and braces. Arms, shoulders, back, and abdomen must be strong to propel a kayak. The fitness benefits of good posture shouldn't be underestimated—it's one of the best abdominal workouts. Sit up straight at work, and take the stairs to the tenth floor. Regular paddling with good paddling posture will strengthen your upper body.

Energetic walking, swimming, or

bike riding will add a great deal to your paddling fitness and overall strength. Have a balanced, well-rounded exercise routine. Kayaking requires a high level of cardiovascular fitness. Although you don't use your legs much in kayaking, they're the best muscles to exercise the heart, since they have the strength and stamina to put a much greater load on the cardiovascular system than you can accomplish using your arms.

A fair downwind breeze will push us along and can be enhanced by setting sails, but there always seems to be plenty of upwind paddling to do. A long two-hour passage is a significant aerobic undertaking. A safe and efficient passage around a headland with turbulent water or across a running tidal current places demands on short-term energy reserves. Breaking out of a surf beach is a high-energy sprint. At the end of the day, when you're most fatigued, the path from the beach back to the car is always uphill—then the kayak has to be hoisted onto the roof rack. The good news is that one of the best ways to improve fitness for paddling is to go out paddling as often as possible—two or three times a week. The bad news is that most of us don't get out that often. There are some not-too-unpleasant things we can do on our off days and during the off season that will lead to greater enjoyment of all aspects of paddling.

To maintain a good level of overall fitness you need to consider strength, power, flexibility, and two energy systems. Strength means having well-developed muscles. Power is the ability to move those muscles quickly. Flexibility lets you move your joints through a full range of motion without undue stress. The aerobic energy system gives the endurance needed for a two-hour paddle. The anaerobic energy system provides for the extra effort of crossing a tidal stream or breaking out of a line of surf.

Flexibility

Warm up before you go paddling. You can warm up by moving all your joints through a full range of motion; "stretching" is not necessary. Pay particular attention to shoulders and arms and hips and waist. Good paddling technique that uses hip, waist, and back muscles will help keep those muscles and joints warm and flexible.

Increasing your flexibility is best done after you're completely warmed up. Hold stretches for several seconds until muscles relax and lengthen. Be gentle and persistent. Yoga and fitness classes will show you how to stretch properly.

Endurance

Go for a brisk walk—swing your arms and get your heart rate up a little—keep going for thirty to forty-five minutes.

Swim laps. It's important to go slowly enough so you can keep going for at least thirty minutes. On day trips, paddle thirty minutes at a steady touring speed of three knots or a little better. Keep your stroke rate up to about thirty strokes a minute (count one side only). On multiday trips, go easy at first. Increase your mileage as the trip proceeds. When starting out on a long trip, begin day one traveling only a few miles. Two five-mile jaunts in one day is a good beginning. On day two add another mile or so. Build up slowly over a week or ten days.

Power and Strength

Strength training needs to be augmented with interval training to increase your power. Your body can be trained to deliver more energy for situations that demand power: breaking out of surf, crossing a tidal race, or catching up to a paddler in need. Interval train while paddling: speed ahead very fast for ten paddle strokes (count one side), then paddle normally until you're fully rested, at least two or three minutes. Then sprint ahead for a count of fifteen. Once again paddle normally until you're fully rested. Then sprint ahead for a count of twenty, rest, sprint ahead for a count of fifteen, rest, then sprint ten and you're done. As you gain power you'll need to increase the number of strokes. The rest phase is important in training your body to develop extra power on demand and then recover quickly, ready to overcome the next challenge.

When you're out for a walk or swim, add another fifteen minutes for interval training. Sprint (or walk very fast, swinging your arms) for thirty seconds or more, then slow down and recover. Cycle through the sprint and rest cycle for fifteen to twenty minutes as described above.

Wrists and Forearms

162 Loosen your grip on your paddle. A grip that is too tight produces excessive wrist stress and can cause pain. This becomes particularly important when you need to paddle in emotionally and physically demanding conditions. Anxiety makes many paddlers take a vise-like white-knuckle grip on the paddle.

163 If you use a feathered paddle and have wrist pain, try reducing the angle of feather. Paddles feathered at ninety degrees sometimes cause wrist problems. Many paddlers are choosing paddles feathered at sixty degrees or less.

164 To prevent or treat blisters on hands, wear inexpensive cotton glove liners. You can buy them at stores that sell work boots and hard hats.

Shoulder Care and Maintenance

The magnificently supple shoulder joint transmits the energy from the paddle blade to the kayak. Shoulders have the greatest range of motion of any joint in the body. The shoulder's only skeletal attachment to the body is where the clavicle (collarbone) attaches to the sternum (breastbone) and runs out to its attachment with the scapula (shoulder blade).

To prevent the significant trauma of shoulder injury, paddlers must have good paddling technique and strong, well-balanced shoulder muscles. For both a low brace and a high brace (that includes rolling), keep your elbows in. Extending your arm and reaching back is a recipe for disaster. The most vulnerable posture, inviting shoulder dislocation, is with the elbow shoulder-high and behind your ear—as if you were reaching into the backseat while driving a car. If your arm does get extended—and this is common—recover to a good elbows-in posture and apply effort to your bracing action by driving your elbow down and in toward your body. This action uses your strong upper arm muscles and puts your shoulder muscles in a safe and strong position. In a low brace, keep your elbows above the paddle and your forearms pointing down in a push-up position.

165 Diligently practice good paddling technique that keeps your elbows low and close to your body. Shoulder dislocation is the injury most likely to incapacitate a paddler. Disable your shoulder and you won't be paddling anywhere for at least several weeks.

166 Keep your paddle blade in sight. Your aft paddle blade should be forward of a line drawn through your shoulders. To place the blade behind the cockpit, turn your body at the waist. Learning to turn your body will protect your shoulders and will also improve your paddling efficiency.

167 Practice very good paddling technique. Whatever you do during practice is what you'll do in a quick

It's important for performance and safety to rotate your torso when paddling to the rear.

response to a steep breaking wave. Very good technique practiced on a calm day will lead to safe technique on a rough day.

Lower Back

Given the choice between a large padded seatback and good posture, choose good posture every time. A small lumbar back strap is often sufficient support for long hours of touring. Good posture is excellent exercise for abdominal muscles, and good fitness will let you maintain good posture. (It's one of those chicken-and-egg things.) A proper seat augmented with hip, thigh, and knee braces and properly adjusted footrests will allow you to sit up with a slight forward lean and keep excellent posture. You'll paddle farther, faster, and longer and suffer less stress on your back.

Good forward paddling technique includes a measure of trunk rotation. Good posture and mild twisting as you paddle will keep your back warmer and ready for any more energetic demands like a quick high brace or sudden roll. **168** Warm up your back before paddling. Many paddle strokes, such as a reverse sweep, stern rudder, and most rolling techniques require you to twist and lean back. A cold, stiff back will rebel against such treatment with mus-

cle spasms or the painful, sometimes debilitating effects of an injured sciatic nerve. Warm up your back by gently flexing your torso left, right, front, and back. Include some gentle torso twists with smooth, continuous motions. **169** Practice yoga. Preventing lower back, wrist, and shoulder injuries can start with a good warm-up with yoga-style exercises.

Warming Up in Your Kayak

- Holding the paddle in a natural position, lean forward and push the paddle toward the bow.
- Assume the roll setup position, first on one side and then on the other.
- Holding the paddle in a natural position, gently rotate your torso and hold the paddle over the side of the kayak parallel to the keel; drop the paddle—it should fall into the water without touching the kayak.
- Holding the paddle with as wide a grip as possible, paddle forward for one minute, then paddle backward for one minute.
- Paddle forward and back with crossover strokes (using the left blade on the right side and the right blade on the left side).

CHAPTER 4

NAVIGATION AND SAFETY

*O*nce you paddle away from the beach you'll need to find your way back. Navigation is more than determining position, course, and speed of travel: the navigator must also be able to communicate that information. Furthermore, in a frail, slow-moving kayak, the shortest route is often not the safest or quickest. In inshore waters, wind and sea conditions can vary greatly from conditions only hundreds of yards away. Strong tidal streams can create large countercurrents, and winds and waves can rebound off steep cliffs. The kayak navigator's skill is part science and part art. Measuring time, distance, and speed is the science of navigation; choosing an efficient route is the art— a matter of judgment and experience. The paddler is both navigator and pilot, responsible for a safe passage out to sea and back again.

170 Check to see that your kayak and other equipment meet regulations for small boats. Double-check the local regulations if you're crossing any borders during your trip.

171 Keep a plastic scuba diver's underwater slate on deck as a log and record critical navigation information. You can also note good fishing conditions or unusual tide rips, reconstruct a narrative of the journey, or develop an understanding of local weather patterns. Paper and pencil do not stand up to conditions on the water, and a log stowed away in a bag or under a hatch is not readily accessible. The slate is impervious to water and is reusable.

172 Rite in the Rain notebooks use water-repellent paper that lets you write in even the wettest conditions.

173 In many areas topographical charts give better detail than marine charts, but be cautious about the differences between the two. Charts are measured in nautical miles and have a compass rose to show declination directly. Maps show only true north and are measured in statute miles in the United States and kilometers in Canada. Maps do not show water depth or currents.

174 While you're paddling, occasionally note what compass direction you're heading. When the fog rolls in you'll know where you've come from and will be able to figure out where you need to get to.

175 Look at charts to see where you'll be crossing shallow water. Waves and current will be exaggerated in shallow areas.

176 Use large-scale charts whenever possible: 1:40,000 shows good detail for kayak navigation.

177 Tidal current predictions are for major waterways well away from shore. Traveling close to shore in a kayak, you can be in much greater or lesser current. In some cases currents near shore form back eddies running opposite to the predominant flow.

178 Currents, waves, and wind in the vicinity of a headland will be greater than those surrounding the area.

Being Heard

Being able to listen in on the latest marine weather forecast may keep you safely ashore, but you may not get to your destination on time. If you can call home and let people know you won't be back till morning, you can prevent an unnecessary rescue call. If you do need help right away, you'll need to communicate with someone. "Always wear a PFD" is an accepted piece of sound advice; but consider being in the water and not being able to tell anyone you need help and where you are. Communication is as important to your safety as flotation.

179 Carry a whistle on your PFD to get attention over short distances. Test your whistle on a windy day when your paddling partner is upwind, well out in front of you.

180 Handheld foghorns are effective, since low-frequency sounds penetrate fog much better than higher-frequency sounds. Have one on hand if fog is a likely hazard.

181 Air-powered horns are really loud. Carefully check the valves for corrosion and leaks. You may seldom need a foghorn, but as with most safety gear, when you do you'll really want it to work.

182 If you need to call out on your radio, do it before you head in to the beach. Handheld 6-watt marine radios can transmit out ten miles or more. (See pages 18–20 on VHF radios and cell phones.) Radio communications are often more effective while at sea. VHF radios transmit in a line-of-sight range. When you're camped on the beach with high ground close behind you, even nearby receivers may be out of sight.

183 Agree on a time to monitor VHF radio transmissions. If paddlers are not back on time, check your radio from five minutes before the hour until five minutes after. Be very flexible when arranging phone or rendezvous times. Too rigid a schedule may put pressure on you to get there, pushing you to travel in marginal weather or stay out to make more miles when you're tired.

Being Seen

One of the first requests of coast guard search-and-rescue teams is that all boaters and boats be clearly visible. Rescues often occur near the end of the day when paddlers are overdue and are getting tired and hungry. The light is fading, and the evening weather is beginning to change. Kayaks are low in the water and difficult to spot from a rescue boat. From the air, spotters in a helicopter are looking for a tiny speck. High-powered lights used in rescues will light up any reflective surface.

184 The color of your boat and equipment are important safety features. In rescue situations, being easy to spot is critical. Yellow or orange is highly visible and efficiently reflects available light in the widest variety of circumstances. Robin's-egg blue is bright and luminescent, so it can be highly visible. Although white provides good contrast, it's not very visible; on a windswept day a plain white hull looks just like a whitecap.

185 Bright-colored and reflective gear is easier for you to find. Stumbling around camp in the dark, you're more likely to see a yellow bag than a dark blue one. When leaving a campsite you're also less likely to miss a bright blue bag on shore than a dark green one.

186 It's important to arrange a few signals that are understood by all members of your group. Include sight, sound, and electronic means of alerting others by day and night.

187 Carry at least two polyethylene survival bags. Large orange plastic survival bags are good (see pages 57–58). They keep out the wind better than wrapping a Mylar survival blanket over your shoulders, and they fold down small enough to be carried almost anywhere.

188 Light sticks are a great source of supplemental light. They're easy to store and pack into various places. Carry one in your PFD, first-aid kit, bailout pack (see pages 54–57), and general camp supplies. Fresh light sticks last for many hours, but old ones can be quite dim. If you handle them too roughly, the internal glass vial can break and you might not realize the light is exhausted.

Replace light sticks each year. Use the new ones for safety purposes; last year's can be used up in camp.

189 Fully submersible flashlights are sold at specialty diving stores. These durable, high-output flashlights come in many sizes and are worth the price.

190 High-output flashlight bulbs run batteries down quickly. Standard bulbs and alkaline batteries serve best for long trips.

191 Get a waterproof headlamp to use while paddling and around camp.

192 Waterproof strobe lights attached to your PFD will signal your distress for a great distance.

Reflective Tape

Small patches of reflective tape are often the first things search-and-rescue teams spot when searching for a paddler. Weatherproof reflective tape is available at yachting supply stores and bike shops. Tape in bulk off a roll is much less expensive than precut packages.

193 Your kayak is a large surface just begging to be adorned. A line of tape around the sheer line looks great. Putting a strip or two down the top center of the deck is very racy. Don't forget to stick some colored reflective tape on the bottom of your hull.

194 Brighten up your paddle blades. While you're paddling your kayak, they're the most prominent features. Your paddle can be used for signaling and for helping others keep track of you. Coast guard launches and helicopters use high-powered searchlights; finding a luminescent paddle can lead them to the unfortunate paddler nearby. Run a line of tape down the length of each blade, on both sides.

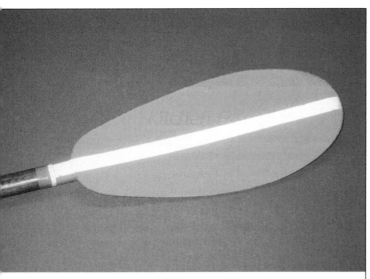

Paddle with reflective tape.

195 On plastic kayaks where tape won't stick, sew reflective tape onto 1-inch tubular nylon webbing and slide the webbing over the deck lines. Make reflective straps that fit across your kayak from side to side and fasten them around the deck lines.

196 Put reflective tape on the shoulders of your PFD, paddle float, and helmet, and make some armbands.

197 A reflective flag fluttering from a small mast on your back deck greatly increases your visibility without interfering with paddling.

Night Paddling

198 Wear a headlamp at night so you can keep your hands on your paddle. Leave it turned off as much as possible to preserve your night vision.

199 You may need to rely heavily on your compass for navigation at night. Some deck-mounted compasses come with a small red night-light; most have glowing numbers or needles. Charge up the phosphorus by shining a bright light directly on it before you leave the beach.

200 Fasten a blue light stick to the collar of your PFD or tape one to a mast. The cool light will not impair your partners' night vision but will keep you visible. Don't use white, red, or green lights on your kayak; other boaters may confuse them with navigation markers or a boat's running lights.

201 Prepare your eyes for night vision. It takes approximately five minutes for your eyes to adjust to low light levels, but it takes only a second for your night vision to be compromised by a bright light in your eyes. Shine flashlights and headlamps well away from your fellow paddlers. It takes thirty minutes for your eyes to adjust to see colors at night. Use a red light around camp before you leave to help you see without degrading your night vision.

202 At night, stay clear of navigable waterways; stay inshore as much as possible. Boaters will not be expecting kayaks out at night.

203 Assign a number to each paddler. The leader is number one. When the leader calls out "One," the others count off in order. It's a simple way to keep track of each other.

204 Taping a light stick to a paddle blade or the end of the shaft will greatly improve the range of a signal.

205 Smoke flares and dye markers are excellent signaling devices designed for marine use during the daytime. Coast guard rescue teams use infrared spotting scopes that can detect minute changes in temperature, so both smoke and dye can show up at night.

206 As a distress signal, you need to fire two single rocket flares within twenty seconds. Try to buy flares that are preloaded with a double shot—one flare produces two rockets. Inexpensive single-shot flares have been reported to fail as often as 50 percent of the time.

207 Rocket flares are best used to pinpoint your location. Call for help on your VHF radio, and when you hear the helicopter or the rescue boat, fire a flare.

208 Modify a light stick. Tie a 6-foot length of string or braided fishing line to one end and make a loop 2½ inches long on the other end of the line. Wrap the line snugly and neatly around the light and fit it back into the package. Fold over the packaging and tape it shut with masking tape, leaving the loop protruding at one side. When you need a rescue, call the coast guard on your VHF radio. Rip open the light stick by pulling on the loop; it will easily tear the masking tape. When you hear the distant sound of the cutter or the helicopter, swing the light in a 12-foot circle overhead. You'll be visible for a long way.

Rescue Gear

If you paddle far enough or long enough you'll eventually be thrown a curve. Having the right equipment and knowing how to use it can reduce a potential disaster to an inconvenience. Practice rescue scenarios before you find yourself in one. Frequently check rescue equipment for wear and tear, and bring it along even when you don't think you'll need it.

209 Paddle with partners who are well trained and well equipped. Most of their rescue gear is for you. Who will they throw their floating lines to? Their hand pumps might be used to pump out your kayak, and their VHF radios can call for help when you are in distress. Your safety is partly determined by the preparedness of your partners.

Towlines

Towing is useful in many circumstances. The need for a rescue can be avoided by towing a slow paddler out of a busy shipping channel or keeping a weak paddler from being blown onto a rocky shore. A tow will soon bring a fatigued, injured, or seasick partner safely ashore. In open-water rescue scenarios, a towline can be a great help in towing a kayak outside a line of surf or across a tide race.

Safety note: Any loose line on the deck of a kayak can be a hazard. A line fastened to a heavy disabled kayak is a serious safety concern. Learn to handle towlines in a class with an instructor or from an experienced paddler before you use one for a rescue. A towline should:

- be quick and simple to use
- deploy without snagging or tangling
- be compact enough to take on every trip
- be easy to release in an emergency

  You can store your towline:

- in the large front pocket of your PFD
- in a deck bag on the front deck where it's easy to reach or on the back deck out of your way
- in a tow belt around your waist; there are many models of tow belts at kayaking stores

210 Buoyant braided ¼-inch line is common for towlines. Floats must be attached to the line to compensate for the weight of the fittings added to the ends.

211 When repacking a towline or throw line, stuff the line into the bag a few feet at a time. Don't coil or fold it. If the line is stuffed into the bag it will come out as it went in, free of kinks and tangles.

212 One length of towline will not fit all applications. A long one can be daisy-chained to shorten it up to about one-third its original length (see appendix, page 126). A stainless steel marine gate hook will keep the chain from unraveling. The person towing can unfasten the hook, unravel some more length, and refasten the hook to secure the towline at its new length.

213 Any towing system must be equipped with a reliable quick release.

214 Deck fittings intended to anchor a towline will be subject to a lot of stress and must be securely bolted through a strong deck. To distribute the load, place a backing plate under the deck beneath the deck fitting.

215 Clear the deck for a safe tow. Towlines attached to quick-release belts around the paddler's waist or fastened to deck fittings will lie along the deck and are apt to get caught up on anything stored on deck.

216 When you're towing for a long time, quick-release tow belts can be worn on the chest. From this position the line has less tendency to get caught up on deck. Towing from the chest can be more comfortable than towing from a point low on your waist.

217 Buy stainless steel carabiners, clips, and hooks made for marine use.

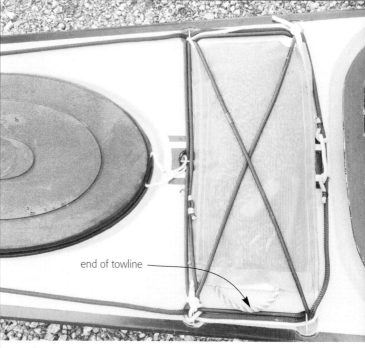

end of towline

Towline stowed on deck.

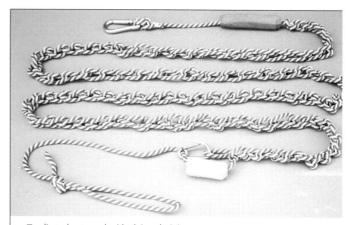

Towline shortened with daisy-chaining.

Those not specifically designed for boats often include other types of metal and will corrode rapidly in salt water. Good hardware made for the purpose is expensive but will function safely for a very long time.

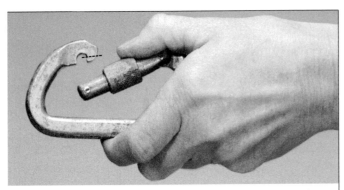

The dashed line above shows where to file a notched carabiner to make a smooth gate.

218 Carabiners should have smooth gates. Notches joining the hook and the gate will get caught on lines, interfering with quick attachment and release. When you try to release a notched carabiner fastened to a loop on your PFD, it will often catch on the loop. File off the hook to make for smooth operation. This does weaken the carabiner, however.

219 If you're offered a tow, you probably need one. Relax, don't be too self-conscious, and accept the offer graciously. There's no shame in taking some help.

220 If someone else needs a tow, offer your help in such a way that the person in need can accept without embarrassment. Encourage the other kayaker to paddle while being towed. People often feel there's a stigma attached to being towed. There needn't be; towing is a means of keeping the group moving.

Paddle Floats

Inflatable paddle floats are easy to carry in the cockpit. The paddle float you bring along is better than the one left at home. When conditions demand more buoyancy, you'll be glad to have at least one.

221 To form a seal between cold lips and the inflation tube of a paddle float or other inflatable device, grasp the tube between your thumb and forefinger and put both fingers and tube in your mouth. The fingers will seal the corners of your lips, which don't pucker very well when cold.

Make Your Own Rigid Paddle Float

You can make a rigid paddle float with a few readily available materials. Rigid paddle floats don't require any inflating or setup. They can be slipped over the paddle quickly and will stay in place if they fit snugly. You'll need:

- 1-inch-thick white polyurethane foam (it comes in two densities; use the higher density if available)
- yellow electrician's tape
- 3/16-inch braided nylon line
- reflective tape

Cut two rectangular pieces of 1-inch-thick rigid foam to match the length and width of your paddle blade. Make a sandwich of these two pieces. Bevel the inner edges of both ends very slightly so the blade can slip between them easily. Cut one more piece of foam the length of the sandwich. Cut two 2-

Rigid paddle float.

inch-wide strips and place them along the outer edges of the sandwich. Bevel the outer edges of the foam and wrap the entire bundle neatly with yellow electrician's tape to bind the four pieces together, leaving both ends open. Add some reflective tape and your name for identification. Pierce a hole near one corner of the float and thread a length of line through it.

222 Keep your paddle float accessible. On the back deck it's out of the way. Nylon straps work better than bungee cords for a secure fastening. Remember that a deck cluttered with too much equipment can be troublesome in a rescue situation.

223 Doing a reentry and roll after a wet exit is easier with a rigid float on the paddle. While you're in the water, remove the float from its storage place on the kayak and slip it over the paddle blade. Reenter your kayak, set up, and roll up. The buoyancy of the float will keep your paddle on the surface and almost ensure a successful roll.

224 Use a rigid paddle float as a training aid while learning to brace and roll. The flat surfaces work like a blade as the paddle sweeps through the water. An inflatable float is round and doesn't plane through the water.

225 A rigid paddle float can be left on as you continue to paddle ahead or will help maintain stability so you can pump out your cockpit before moving on.

226 At home, store your rigid paddle float where it will dry thoroughly. Insert a broom handle down the middle to let air circulate and promote drying.

227 Avoid sitting or standing on your paddle float. The pressure crushes the cells and lets water infiltrate the foam.

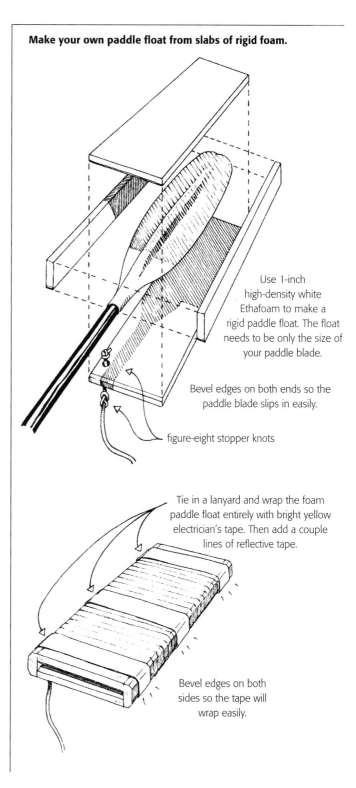

Make your own paddle float from slabs of rigid foam.

Use 1-inch high-density white Ethafoam to make a rigid paddle float. The float needs to be only the size of your paddle blade.

Bevel edges on both ends so the paddle blade slips in easily.

figure-eight stopper knots

Tie in a lanyard and wrap the foam paddle float entirely with bright yellow electrician's tape. Then add a couple lines of reflective tape.

Bevel edges on both sides so the tape will wrap easily.

Cockpit rescue stirrup.

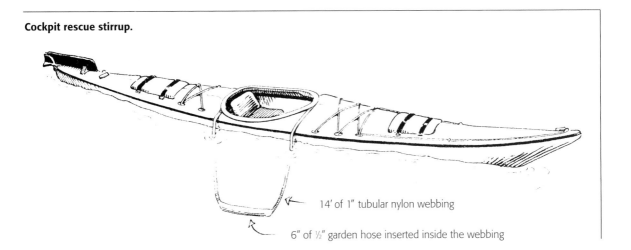

14' of 1" tubular nylon webbing

6" of ½" garden hose inserted inside the webbing

Rescue Stirrup

Some paddlers find it impossible to reenter a kayak with a high back deck. Fatigue or hypothermia may disable an otherwise proficient paddler trying to get back into the kayak. A rescue stirrup can be a necessary leg up. Cut a piece of 1-inch nylon tubular webbing long enough (about 14 feet) to reach around the cockpit coaming and hang 18 inches into the water. Push 6 inches of garden hose through the tubing up to the midpoint to create an open step in the flexible webbing. The webbing can be tied into a loop the correct length for the boat, the person, and the technique being used. Remember that much of your gear might be used to rescue someone else.

228 If you can't climb into your own kayak, climb onto your rescuer's boat first. Push the stern down and scramble onto the deck. The rescuer holds your boat steady while you scramble over to your own boat.

Signal Mirror

Mirrors have long been recognized as effective signaling devices. In his circumnavigation of Australia, described in *Dreamtime Voyage*, Paul Caffyn used a signal mirror to communicate with his shore crew. They directed him to safe passages through the surf by mirror flashes.

A Mayday signal mirror is reflective on both sides with a hole in the center to sight through. Have one as part of your safety gear. The sparkling image is visible to a target miles away. Practice aiming it when onshore. If you ever need it, you'll have to know how to use it (see illustration, page 55).

Bailout Pack

If at all possible, stay in your kayak. But if circumstances force you to bail out, your chances are improved by thoughtful preparation. A bailout pack will extend a swimmer's survival time.

A bailout pack is needed when the paddler is at least temporarily separated from the kayak and becomes a survival swimmer. Its contents must meet the

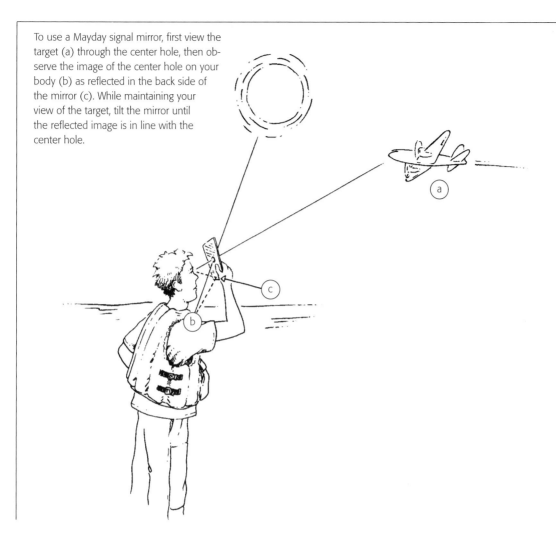

To use a Mayday signal mirror, first view the target (a) through the center hole, then observe the image of the center hole on your body (b) as reflected in the back side of the mirror (c). While maintaining your view of the target, tilt the mirror until the reflected image is in line with the center hole.

specific needs of the paddling environment. When you're paddling in Fiji, fresh water would take priority over fire-making supplies. In Alaska, fresh water may be readily available but warmth may be hard to find. A bailout pack must be

- worn by the paddler
- secure and unobtrusive
- able to float
- large enough to hold the necessary equipment

- small enough not to be a hindrance

The equipment it contains must help the paddler

- remain buoyant
- communicate with rescuers
- reenter the kayak in a rough sea
- keep warm in cold water
- survive when ashore without a kayak

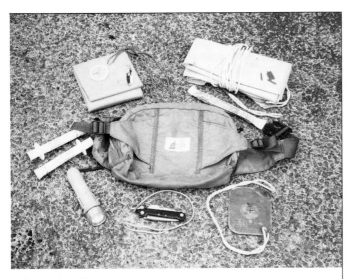
Bailout pack and its contents.

- emergency food bars
- fishing tackle
- Mylar survival blanket

The pack can be a standard good-quality hiker's fanny pack. Fabric, zippers, and buckles need to stand up to the rigors of the marine environment. Additional D-rings can be sewn inside the pack to secure the contents. I've also seen custom-made neoprene fanny packs with watertight (dry suit) zippers. When you load the pack, use Ziploc bags, plastic film canisters, lanyards, and the like to protect items from being lost or damaged at sea.

The bailout pack should be well maintained. Remove and inspect the contents after each trip. Dry everything out and check for deterioration and water infiltration. Each year, replace light sticks, first-aid supplies, and other items that may degrade. Be aware of expiration dates on flares.

Now that you have all the equipment nicely stored away in your new pack, you need to decide where to keep it. To be reasonable, you don't wear it every time you sit in your kayak. There are three unequal choices:

- **Behind your seat.** This is suitable when the likelihood of needing the pack is zero, such as on a summer day paddle along a sheltered beach with friends. Placed here, the pack is secure and dry but hard to reach.
- **On the foredeck.** The pack's belt will attach securely to deck lines. This is an appropriate place for moderate sea states or touring inshore in good weather where conditions change slowly. Placed here, the pack is easy to reach and put

These rather demanding requirements can be met with an 8-quart (13 by 8 by 5 inches, about 500 cubic inches) fanny pack containing a well-thought-out collection of equipment. The following list reflects the needs of a paddler in the wilderness areas on the temperate west coast of North America:

- rigid foam to keep the pack afloat
- identification, money, credit card
- orange plastic survival bags
- first-aid kit
- compass
- signal mirror
- rocket flares
- smoke flares
- light stick
- whistle
- flashlight
- knife
- waterproof matches
- candles; wax fire starters
- inflatable flotation device

Bailout pack worn around the waist.

on if conditions change but vulnerable to being swept away.

- **Around your waist.** The pack must be worn to be effective. When paddling exposed coastlines near surf or heavy tide races, where conditions can change quickly and dramatically, you should wear the pack at all times. Belt loops on your PFD help keep the pack from slipping off.

Orange Plastic Bags

I mean really big plastic survival bags. In typical plastic bag fashion, these giants fold down to minuscule proportions. They have a great many uses and are a must to take along. (They're available from Coghlan's Ltd., 121 Irene St., Winnipeg MB, R3T 4C7 Canada; 204-284-9550; or look

Bailout pack fastened to the foredeck.

in the Sleeping Bag section of www.outdoorworldca.com.)

229 Loading and unloading the contents of your kayak into a couple of big plastic or mesh bags means fewer trips to and from the beach.

230 One large bag can be used as a compartment liner. If you have a slightly leaky hatch cover, put a large bag in the hatch and fill it with your

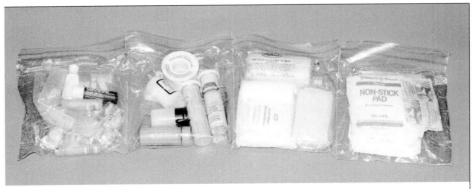

First-aid kit made by taping Ziploc bags together.

stuff. This works particularly well for the smaller loads carried on a day trip.

231 Need emergency rain gear? Cut a slit for your head and two armholes and you're covered.

232 One bag cut open can serve as a minitarp. Cover what dry firewood you have. Cover the leaky corner on your tent. Build a lean-to.

233 Use one as an emergency bivvy sack to keep your sleeping bag dry or inside a wet sleeping bag to keep you dry.

234 A large orange plastic bag blown up like a balloon makes a good signaling device.

235 Cracked and leaking kayaks can be jury-rigged by wrapping them in plastic. Packing tape applied to a dry surface holds up well when wet.

First-Aid Kit

236 Use clear packing tape to fasten several Ziploc bags together. Individual bags keep supplies nicely organized and easy to find. Together, the collection of bags becomes a complete first-aid kit.

CHAPTER 5

FOOD AND WATER

*T*o fuel a human-powered craft you need sugar and water and oxygen. Simple sugars (simple carbohydrates) give you a burst of energy but won't sustain any lasting effort. Starches (complex carbohydrates) are more suited for fueling several hours' work. During the paddling day you're better off eating complex carbohydrates rather than protein. Proteins build and repair muscle tissue; save the high-protein foods for the end of the day when they can be metabolized over a longer period. Your body can store enough ready energy for about two hours of paddling. If you run out, your body will break down protein and fat to make fuel, a slower and less efficient process, and you'll tire more quickly. Although carbohydrate-rich snacks can keep you going through the day, you'll still need more fat and protein than usual, particularly when paddling in cool climates.

Fuel for a Human-Powered Craft

237 Plan your meals over a cycle of two or three days and be sure to consider all your dietary needs. Also, it's often revealing to log what you eat for two or three days to see how well you've met your nutritional requirements.

238 Eat well, eat frequently. Your body needs fuel to keep the heat on. Good carbohydrate meals and snacks throughout the day provide ready energy (see Traveling Snacks in the appendix, page 118.) Carbohydrates are metabolized faster than fats or proteins. High-protein and high-fat foods are longer-lasting energy sources; have them at dinner so you can digest them during the night.

239 As soon as you're safely ashore, have a good carbohydrate snack—something that can be packed for easy access, such as a sports bar, a muffin, or a bagel. Drink some more fluid to help you digest it. Keeping your dietary needs constantly met is the most effective way to maintain good fuel burning; a run-down metabolism is hard to restart.

Hydration

What you drink should reflect the type of exercise you're doing. In cool climates where perspiration is light, diluted juices or sports drinks are adequate. Water would be fine, but you'll drink more if the drink is flavored. In warmer conditions or when workloads are high and you're sweating heavily, you must pay attention to replacing salts and other electrolytes as well as fluids. Water supplemented with salty snacks and pieces of fruit is good, but a fruit or sports drink kept on deck is usually more convenient.

240 Drink before you're thirsty. It's easier and more efficient to stay well hydrated than to recover from dehydration. By the time you feel thirsty you're well into being dehydrated. Drink lots, drink often. You'll have more energy, be in a better mood, and make better decisions. You'll digest your snacks better. All around, you'll have a safer and more pleasant paddling day.

241 Once ashore, take a good long drink and eat a healthy snack right away. You can use the boost before the arduous task of unloading all the gear and making camp. You'll enjoy your higher fat and protein dinner more if you're not ravenous, and you'll digest it better.

242 Keep a flask handy. A small curved plastic flask with a low profile fits nicely on the deck and doesn't get washed away as easily as larger cylindrical bottles. But you may get comments.

243 You need almost as much fluid on cold days as on hot days, but you may be less aware of thirst. Dehydration hastens hypothermia.

244 Hydration systems are available that fasten to your PFD. Other types can be secured in the cockpit.

Guidelines for Fluid Consumption

- 16 ounces in the morning
- 8 ounces every thirty minutes
- something to drink with every meal and every snack
- 2 to 4 quarts each day (monitor your consumption)

245 Avoid alcohol and caffeine. Both increase peripheral circulation and will end up cooling you down. A hot, sweet drink such as peppermint tea with sugar will warm you better. If you're cold, anything warm will taste good.

Now that you have all this fluid coursing through your body, you'll eventually have to get rid of some of it.

246 Men can pee into a small container, sponge, or Ziploc bag. It's more inconvenient for women. The Sani-fem is a device to funnel urine into a bottle or sponge like the fellows use. (It's made by Freshette, P.O. Box 4117, Downey CA 90241; 219-268-0081.)

247 Pee by the clock—plan your day to accommodate yourself.

248 Avoid caffeine and alcohol before long spells of sitting in your kayak. They're both diuretics that will increase urine output so you'll need to pee more often.

Conserving Water

Water is everywhere, but at sea in a kayak there may not be a drop to drink. The ocean can be a thirsty place, and staying strong and healthy demands several quarts of clean water every day. Finding, treating, storing, and transporting water can take a significant amount of time and effort. Using lots of water and conserving what you have are conflicting endeavors. A successful trip needs careful water management.

249 Use salt water for brushing teeth.

250 After a saltwater bath you just need a good toweling off to remove the salty residue. Even your hair will feel clean if thoroughly toweled.

251 Collect the rainwater running off your tarp or use untreated groundwater for bathing. It may contain tannin from the trees, coloring it brown and making it less palatable for drinking, but it will be fine for washing dishes and rinsing off after a saltwater bath.

252 Conserve water and fuel when cooking pasta. Use one-third salt water. Boil the pasta for half the required time and then let it stand off the stove for double the remaining time. Use a tea cozy to keep the pot hot.

253 Cook rice when you're low on water. Pasta water gets thrown out, but the water used to cook rice is completely absorbed.

254 Use a double boiler for rice and pasta and steam the vegetables in the top to save fuel. The top pot helps insulate the bottom pot as well. Use a tea cozy to keep everything warm when off the stove.

255 Fill a thermos with hot water at breakfast: this saves both fuel and time at lunch, since you won't have to unpack the stove. A full thermos stays hotter than a partially filled one.

256 Carefully measure food portions. Leftovers mean wasted food, water, and fuel.

Collecting and Treating Water

A source of clean drinking water, free of bacteria and viruses, is paramount. Many devices are available to filter out pathogens. Using a good-quality filtering system is one step in a comprehensive health management plan, but water filters are only as good as your personal hygiene. Handling the filter outlet or receiving container with dirty hands will contaminate otherwise clean water. The internal workings of the filter not only have to perform properly, they must also be clean. A poorly maintained filter will be a breeding ground for contaminants. Harmful bacteria in groundwater are much less common than dirty hands. When sharing finger foods, it takes only one dirty hand to infect the entire group.

Careless food storage and preparation are another common source of highly toxic contaminants. Knives used for cutting meat, food preparation surfaces, and jars opened but not refrigerated are all hazards.

In populated and industrial areas, don't use groundwater at all. Chemical contaminants from lawn fertilizer and manufacturing can't be filtered out. In these areas, get your water from an established source of public drinking water.

In wilderness areas natural pathogens such as *Giardia* can cause serious infections that may not present symptoms until six weeks later, usually after the trip is over. Exposure to human fecal bacteria, salmonella, and natural toxins found in many marine shellfish (see page 69) will produce debilitating, sometimes deadly, reactions within hours.

257 Leaving water in a clear container in the sun for several hours reduces harmful bacteria and viruses. In the absence of more sophisticated methods, this may be an alternative.

Cook with a double boiler to help conserve fuel.

steaming veggies

boiling pasta

258 Collect water from a small pool formed by a fresh source. The common wisdom of taking water only from running streams may not be so wise, since parasitic cysts and particulate matter are stirred up by moving water. If you can't filter it, collect water in one container and let it stand for a couple of hours, then slowly decant the top two-thirds into clean containers.

259 Catch free-falling rain in a clean tarp under an open sky. (Bird feces and other contaminants collect on tree branches and drip to the ground.)

260 If there's any doubt about germs or parasites, the water must be run through a purification filter. Let turbid water stand, then strain it through a coffee filter to remove most of the particulate matter before using your water purifier; this keeps your pump from clogging.

261 Crystalline iodine stores easily and, if you follow the instructions, is effective in treating water for some contaminants. It does leave a noticeable taste that puts many people off.

262 Chlorine-based water purifiers that use buffered chlorine dioxide are an alternative to more traditional iodine-based purifiers.

263 To treat water, put two or three drops of chlorine bleach in a quart of clear water. Let it stand for an hour or longer. You should be able to smell the chlorine at first, but overnight the odor should go away. Treat colder water and turbid water longer and stronger. Cold temperatures inhibit the chemical reactions responsible for killing pathogens.

Groceries versus Menus versus Recipes

Some paddlers pack meals in individual Ziploc bags numbered for each day, but sea kayaking may be your way to get away from regimentation and routine. Another way to plan for eight nights is to take enough for three dinners with rice, three with pasta, and two with bread, carrots for four dinners, corn for two, green beans for two, cabbage for four, broccoli for two, and tomatoes for two. For each meal have two vegetables and one starch. Complete the rest of the grocery/menu list in the same fashion.

A similar approach is to plan a menu for every meal, then list the groceries you need. Buy all the groceries and leave the menu home.

264 Shop differently for kayaking groceries than you would for eating at home. Small quantities will stay fresh longer. Bread in sealed bags lasts longer than bread fresh off the bakery shelves. Some things in more packaging cost more, but if good packaging prevents spoilage, your food will get eaten rather than thrown out.

265 Keep a food log. List what you took along and what came back, and update your grocery list for next time. After a few trips you'll be able to shop quickly, buying what you'll eat and avoiding waste.

266 For long trips bundle five days' food into one dry bag. After a few days out you'll get to open a new bag and have some of your favorite foods again.

267 Tea and coffee bags are expensive but very handy. Coffee bags simplify brewing. Tea and coffee are biodegradable, but the bags are very durable. Pack them out.

268 Instant cappuccino is a treat; soup mixes or foil-wrapped instant hot drinks may not be staples at home, but few will turn them down when camping on a cool evening.

Kitchen Equipment

A sea kayak can have room for a cutting board, a double boiler, a two-burner stove, and an apple pie. I've even seen a hibachi and a case of beer come out from under an aft hatch. You just might spend as much time cooking, eating, and cleaning up as you do paddling. A well-stocked kitchen can provide a delicious dinner and redeem a difficult day of paddling with a pleasant evening.

Kitchen Essentials

- A backpacker's stove. A good stove should be quiet and fuel efficient, simmer foods well, and be easy to maintain.
- Nesting pots. These are a must; a frypan is handy for fish and tortillas.
- Stainless steel knife and fork and a couple of spoons. A large serving spoon and fork are handy for cooking.
- Can opener, bottle opener, and corkscrew. Combination tools are handy.
- Paring knife. A small, straight serrated blade is easier to work with than a folding knife.
- Cutting board. Small, lightweight synthetic ones are available.
- Insulated mug with a lid. This is a must for keeping hot drinks hot.
- Spatula. For flipping pancakes and eggs.
- Aluminum foil. Bring a couple of good-sized pieces folded up for cooking fish or potatoes in the fire. Some camp cooks take a whole roll.
- Plastic bowls. One should be big enough to make a salad for two. Two nesting bowls take up no

more room than one, and the second can be used as a cover.

- Lexan plates and bowls are sturdy, easy to clean, and have no plastic taste.
- Salt and pepper shakers with sealing lids. For herbs and spices you can use camping containers or small Ziploc bags collected into one larger bag. Glass jars can break, and film canisters may contain chemical contaminants from the film.
- Olive oil or other cooking oil. Oil does seem to migrate onto everything, however; sealing the oil container inside another container will prevent an oily mess.

269 Make kitchen roll-ups. A dish towel folded and stitched to form several pockets will hold cutlery and kitchen utensils.

A kitchen roll-up.

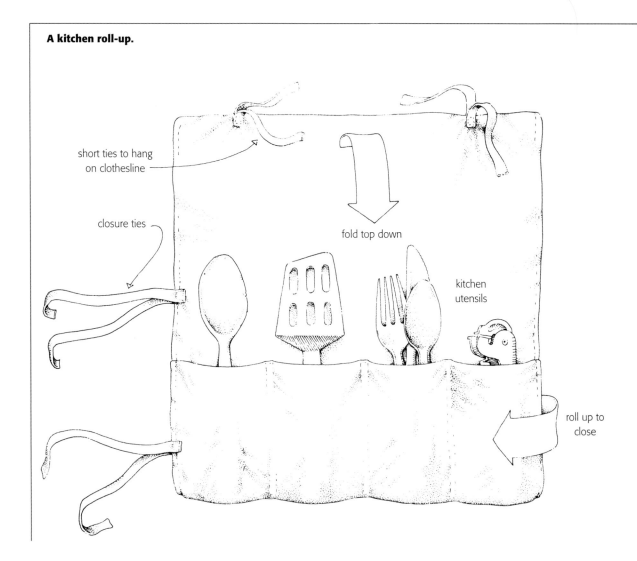

short ties to hang on clothesline

closure ties

fold top down

kitchen utensils

roll up to close

Pots and Pans

- Uncoated aluminum. Inexpensive aluminum cookware has gone out of favor; it dents easily, and food sticks to it. Aluminum oxidizes over time and may be a health hazard.
- Nonstick aluminum. Newer coatings are durable but still need to be handled with some care. Use plastic utensils and wash pots with a cloth or nylon scrubber.
- Stainless steel. Lightweight stainless steel cookware is strong and durable, but it doesn't distribute heat as evenly as aluminum.
- Titanium. Titanium is extremely resilient, light, durable, and clearly the most expensive. Because the metal is so thin, it's energy efficient and distributes heat well.

270 Rounded bottom edges are easier to clean, and heat from the stove is distributed more uniformly up the sides of the pot.

271 Tight-fitting lids are critical to maximize efficiency. The pot will heat faster so you'll use less fuel, and the contents will stay warm longer when off the heat.

272 Look for pots that nest and have folding handles. Loose pot grabbers work well but get lost.

273 Carry a nylon pot scrubber with a sponge on one side and a scouring pad on the other. These amazing little things are useful for cleaning up cookware with delicate nonstick coatings.

274 Liquid hand soap works well for washing dishes, hair, and hands and for bathing. Concentrated liquid camping soap is excellent and usually biodegradable, which is particularly important in freshwater environments.

275 Rinse dishes well. Soap left on dishes frequently causes the digestive upsets blamed on contaminated food, hands, or water.

276 Try cleaning greasy pans with dry rather than wet sand. It's very hard to wash greasy pans in salt water without soap. Don't use sand on your nonstick pans, though.

277 Use a fingernail brush before cooking. Cleanliness is paramount when kayak touring. Sanitary toilet habits are more difficult to maintain, and washing up is more trouble. But the consequences of carelessness are more debilitating away from the comforts of home.

Stoves

Buy a stove that will simmer food well. Almost all stoves produce plenty of heat, but many won't maintain a constant low temperature. If you can't make soup in the stove, you'll have to ask fellow campers about their stoves.

To increase efficiency and save fuel

- use a heat diffuser to aid in simmering
- use a wind screen
- use heat reflectors only on burners with separate fuel tanks
- keep the fuel tank cool; it's the pot you want to heat, not the fuel tank!
- buy a quiet stove
- use the recommended fuel type
- always pack a stove repair kit and spare parts

278 Make a buddy burner. An emergency backup stove can be made with a tuna-fish can, some wax, and a little corrugated cardboard. Stuff the can with rolled-up cardboard and then fill it with melted wax. (See page 93 on melting wax.) Light it once before you leave home; the wax will saturate the cardboard wick so it will be easier to light in the field.

279 Always filter your fuel. Fuel contaminated with particulate matter is a common cause of stove failure.

280 Pack your stove in a rigid container. A billy pot that fits the stove is a handy pairing. It's always good if an item can serve more than one purpose.

281 Keep the fuel cap on tightly when the stove is burning. Refuel your stove only when it's cool. Although this seems obvious, the temptation can be very great just to top up the stove to keep it going.

282 The pot size should fit the stove top. Spilling boiling pasta can be disastrous. A wide-bottomed pot reflects a lot of heat downward, overheating the fuel tank.

Food Storage and Preparation

If you share the cooking, you're effectively sharing personal hygiene practices. The main cause of upset stomachs, diarrhea, and serious gastrointestinal infections is self-contamination owing to poor personal hygiene and spoiled food. Out in the wilderness a bit of sand in your food may be accepted as part of the adventure, but poor hygiene cannot be tolerated. Two major causes for emergency evacuation on wilderness trips are small cuts that get seriously infected and gastrointestinal illness from poor toilet habits.

283 Carry some bleach. Occasionally disinfect cutting boards, bowls, and other utensils. One part bleach in ten parts water will disinfect your kitchen. Concentrated bleach must be stored in a container intended for it; save small bleach sample bottles, which are specially treated to hold caustics.

284 Waterless alcohol-based soaps are antibacterial and easy to use and encourage frequent hand washing—no drying. They can be kept in with kitchen utensils, ready for regular use.

285 When ashore, cover your kayak with a tarp or Mylar survival blanket. Vegetables stored in the bottom of the kayak keep cool while you're paddling, but on shore the temperature will rise. A reflective cover over the kayak will keep your carrots from going limp.

286 No double-dipping: dirty spoons can contaminate jars of jam, salsa, and relish.

287 Take along foil packs of relish, mayonnaise, and salad dressing. Make sure to check their expiration dates.

288 Paper milk cartons double as containers. Bread fits into a two-quart box, and pasta, cucumbers, or cookies fit in a one-quart carton. Once you've eaten the contents, use the cartons as kindling or garbage pack-out containers.

289 Precook a meal for the first night. Often the first day out is hectic, with road travel and other obligations. Preparing your first dinner in advance makes for less work and also lets you have something you likely couldn't cook on a camp stove.

290 Chill or freeze your groceries at home. The car trip to the launch site can overheat all your fresh produce. Before leaving the house, freeze water, juice, and meat. During transport store produce in a cooler and keep the cold items in a cooler or bundled together.

291 Use a straw to suck the air out of plastic bags before you seal them.

292 Double-bagging will keep your bread fresh longer. Slightly compress the bags to expel air.

293 Leave glass jars at home.

294 Preservatives work. At home no preservatives may be the preferred choice, but eight days away from the refrigerator you'll be glad you brought packaged breads.

295 Eat your fresh onion and cheese bagels first. Save the sealed, well-preserved ones for later in the trip.

296 Buy your fruit and vegetables in various stages of ripeness. Half of your tomatoes should be underripe—they'll last longer and be better able to take a little knocking around. Check to see that your produce is clean, dry, and bruise-free.

297 Pita breads, bagels, and other heavy breads withstand rough handling better than softer breads.

298 Once it's open, use it up. Don't open breads and cereal until you need them—keep them dry and in their original containers.

299 Take cereal out of the box before you pack it and put it in a Ziploc bag. Keep it in the airtight waxed paper liner to help keep the cereal crisp.

300 Vegetables should be aired and dried every day or two. Use a clean paper towel to wipe then off, then reuse the towel to clean up spills or start the fire.

301 Eat fish for lunch, not supper. Its smell is sure to attract wildlife like raccoons, otters, and bears. After lunch you can paddle away and leave your clean, slightly fishy smelling campsite behind.

302 Spice your foods. Herbs and spices add a great deal to a simple menu; black pepper and allspice are good standbys. A couple of small jars of hot salsa can perk up all sorts of recipes.

Foraging

Living off the land, even just a little, requires knowledge and experience. The ocean depths and shoreline can yield an abundance of food, both very good and very bad.

Shellfish

Before you leave home, phone fisheries or local health officials and ask about paralytic shellfish poisoning (PSP) and other harmful algal blooms (HABs) where you'll be traveling. If the area is safe you can dine on clams, mussels, or oysters. If you don't get an all clear, don't eat them. If you're not sure, do not eat any shellfish, tropical fish, or other unfamiliar seafood.

PSP, commonly called red tide, is caused by a naturally occurring toxin produced by microscopic algae known as phytoplankton. Filter-feeding animals such as clams, mussels, oysters, snails, scallops, and barnacles eat this plankton, and the toxin builds up in their body tissues.

Occasionally the plankton population increases dramatically. If the population is very large, it will form visible reddish patches near the surface. However, harmful concentrations of this toxic plankton are usually not visible. The tradition that it is safe to eat shellfish during certain months is not reliable; seafood can be contaminated during every month. Some species of clams have been known to be continuously poisonous for years.

People have died after eating just one clam. No simple, reliable test for PSP exists, and most wilderness beaches are not tested.

Signs of PSP may occur within ten to thirty minutes after eating affected seafood. Symptoms include tingling or burning of the lips, gums, tongue, face, neck, arms, legs, and toes, and nausea, vomiting, diarrhea, and abdominal pain. Later problems may include shortness of breath, dry mouth, a choking feeling, confused or slurred speech, and lack of coordination. Make the victim as comfortable as possible and call for medical assistance immediately.

Other HABs also produce toxins that can poison humans. Although these marine organisms occur naturally, excessive nutrients from human-caused pollution may increase algal populations to harmful levels. Other toxins found in marine animals are also directly attributable to human habitation. In this case the pollution problem is secondary to the toxicity.

303 Beware of toxins introduced to the food chain by pulp mills and factory outfalls. Avoid camping or foraging near such industries.

304 To forage safely for marine life, you must be knowledgeable and well informed. Seek out recent local information from a reliable source and obey all posted warnings and fishing closures.

305 Take along a field guide to local wildlife.

306 Generally you can safely collect sea urchins, limpets, abalones, and seaweed.

307 Bring a field guide to edible plants so you can look for the proverbial roots and berries on shore. It takes some knowledge to collect and prepare wild foods, but it will add local flavor to your trip.

308 Carry a few dollars in your kayak. Fishing boats will often sell some of their catch to paddlers, and they may be also a source of fresh water and fuel. Yachts often have alcohol stoves and can usually spare a pint of fuel.

Fishing

There's a bumper sticker that says "a bad day's fishing is better than a good day's work." Freshly caught fish cooked over the open fire is a goal worth pursuing. Unfortunately, some fish species are poisonous and others must be caught during a limited season. Check local fisheries regulations before you go.

309 Any fishing line attached to the kayak must have a quick release. You just might hook a large bottom fish capable of taking you on an unexpected adventure.

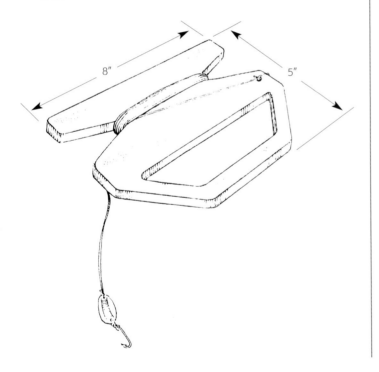

Basic fishing tackle: a hand line made from ⅜-inch marine-grade plywood. Use a weighted spoon so you can troll behind the kayak while you're moving or fish the bottom as you float near the edge of a kelp bed or reef.

8"

5"

A little time spent with a hand line and hook along the edge of a kelp bed provided supper for three.

310 Braided cod line is durable and doesn't tangle into a bird's nest the way monofilament does. It's also useful for odd jobs. You might want a glove to protect your hand when pulling in the big one.

311 Use plain steel hooks and keep them sharp with a small file. Stainless steel hooks don't rust; a common steel hook will deteriorate quickly, so a fish that gets away will fare much better.

312 Consider what kind of fish you want to bring on board. Leave small sharks—or big ones for that matter—in the water. Even small dogfish sharks can deliver painful puncture wounds with their tail spines.

313 Keep your catch and keep it fresh. A simple gill line or stringer lets the fish trail in the water. You can make one with a short stick and a piece of line.

314 Carry some flexible wire so you can tie your fish to a couple of sticks and cook it over an open fire.

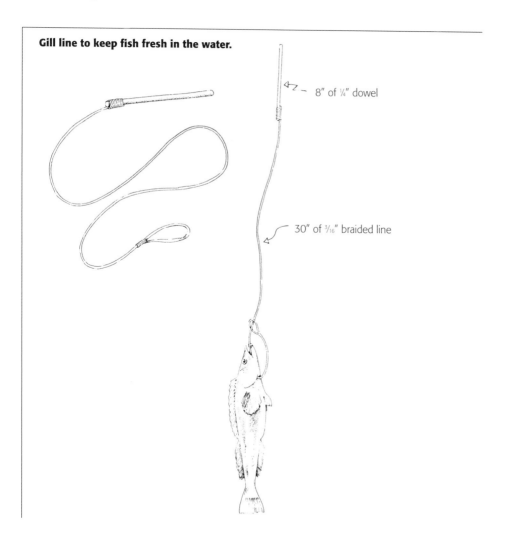

Gill line to keep fish fresh in the water.

8" of ¼" dowel

30" of ³⁄₁₆" braided line

CHAPTER 6

CLOTHING

Choosing what to wear is one of the toughest decisions in sea kayaking. The transition from dry and warm to wet and cold can be instantaneous. More often though, you're warm while paddling but quickly get chilled once ashore. You can stay dry under a waterproof hat, inside a high-tech waterproof-breathable paddling jacket, and sealed inside your kayak with a snug sprayskirt. Paddling keeps you warm. Roll your kayak over, and by and large you stay dry. But step ashore in the rain for a lunch break and you'll get wet and cold. On a sunny day in high latitudes the water stays cold, and the potential for immersion is always a wet exit away. Deciding what to wear is critical to both comfort and safety.

Fabric Choices

Modern fabrics and clothing designed for outdoor enthusiasts have evolved well beyond the melton cloth pants, oilskins, and high boots of the sailor's distant past.

When shopping for those expensive outdoor garments, check the quality carefully. One of the prime determinants of cost is the item's technical construction. Both inexpensive and costly rainwear may be made of the same fabric. The more expensive version should have taped seams that are double-sewn or heat sealed (or both). Better design and construction will let a garment breathe through zippered armpit vents or open pleats. Zippers will be backed up with flaps to prevent drafts.

Look for garments that will pack down small. There's significant variation in how much garments can be compressed, particularly rainwear.

Cotton

Cotton gets wet and stays wet. If it's wet with salt water, it will pull more moisture out of the air and can be very hard to dry without a freshwater rinse. Wet cotton can keep you cool in the hot sun, but it doesn't protect you from sunburn. Cotton garments are best left at home.

Wool

Although wool gets wet and stays wet, it still keeps you warm. But have you ever worn wet wool for very long? It's very hard to get it dry, and nearly impossible if it's wet with salt water. Wool takes up a lot of room when you're packing.

Polyester

Polyester is most commonly seen as fleece. It gets wet but the water quickly drains out, and it can be squeezed almost dry. Polyester worn next to your body quickly gets smelly. A midweight fleece sweater and pants are easily compressed, taking up very little space when you pack.

Polypropylene

Often used in underwear because it wicks moisture away from sweaty bodies, polypropylene dries quickly but gets very smelly very fast.

Nylon

When layered over fleece or other thermal layers, nylon adds wind resistance and a fair degree of waterproofing. Wet nylon pants will not transfer much moisture to fleece undergarments. New nylon weaves are very comfortable; they dry very quickly, and they're cool when worn as a single layer. Nylon shorts are a must. Like all synthetics, nylon shirts worn next to the skin quickly get smelly, but they wash and dry like a dream. Nylon garments pack down to take hardly any space.

NATURAL MATERIALS

A small crowd gathered at the mouth of the Mackenzie River in the Yukon Territory to watch a demonstration by Greenland's current national rolling champion. His sealskin kayak was a technological wonder thousands of years old. It creaked and flexed as he slipped in. He wore an Eskimo *tuiliq*, a one-piece hooded dry top and sprayskirt. Like his kayak, the waterproof jacket was made of sealskin. His *tuiliq*, like the high-tech dry tops of today, had to be well maintained to stay watertight. "You have to rub it down with blubber a couple of times each year," he said. "It doesn't smell so good, but it keeps the water out."

Breathable Outer Layers

Salt quickly interferes with the function of many multilayer breathable fabrics. Although they're superior in camp, they're hard to maintain on salt water. Fabrics are constantly improving; the best waterproof-breathable saltwater paddling tops remain very expensive but can be worth it. Money can't buy you happiness, but it can buy you comfort!

315 In cold, wet climates buy heavier waterproof-nonbreathable rainwear. In a deluge 100 percent waterproof outers are a must. Kayakers are usually not working or hiking hard in their rain gear; keeping dry in camp is a primary consideration. Warm, wet climates, particularly if you're working hard, place more difficult demands on rain gear.

316 The longer your trip, the less clothing you should take so you can leave room for other gear. Seasoned sea kayakers take a set of clothes to paddle in and a set to wear in camp. Add good rain gear and some extra quick-dry socks and undershirts.

317 Change your socks and undershirt daily. When you're feeling grimy, fresh socks and shirt are almost as good as a hot shower. Wash them thoroughly after each wearing, rinse extra well, and dry them quickly to inhibit odors. Washing stinky synthetics with deodorant soap helps minimize odor.

318 Wash residual sunscreen and bug dope off at the end of each day.

319 Wear sock liners in your sandals in the kayak or when walking on the beach. Sand or small stones caught under the straps cause painful abrasions that are slow to heal. Sock liners are light and dry very quickly. Wearing them with your sandals may not be a fashion statement, but it will save your feet some abuse.

320 Power dry your fleece clothing. Viscose camper's towels absorb 2,000 percent of their own weight in water; polyester fleece absorbs 0.5 percent of its weight. If you layer a dry towel and wet fleece together and wring them out, the water will move out of the fleece and into the towel. Wring out the towel and repeat the process a couple of times. The fleece will end up almost dry.

321 Layer your clothing. Wearing an outer layer of high-durability nylon and an under layer of warm polyester fleece works very well.

322 When out touring, take along two paddling jackets. A good-quality loose-fitting paddling top with nonwatertight wrist and neck closures makes an excellent rain jacket and windbreaker around camp. Layer it with a mid-weight fleece for warmth.

323 Drying synthetic garments near a fire is hazardous. Even if the sparks don't produce instant holes, the woven fibers will be weakened and disintegrate later in the wash.

Fabric Care

Modern fabrics are a marvel of space-age engineering. Waterproof and waterproof-breathable fabrics are now a mainstay of sea kayaking paraphernalia. In some cases our lives depend on fabric technology. As with any technology, however, maintenance and repair are an ongoing concern. With care, dry suits, wet suits, tents, and tarps will perform their functions for many years.

324 Even after a day trip you need to rinse out your gear. Buy a large plastic garbage can. When you get home and unload the car, drop all your paddling gear into the can, fill it with water, and slosh vigorously. A small hole in the bottom will let the water drain slowly enough to give your gear a soak. Hang things out to dry before you go to bed.

325 Once you're home from a trip, wash all equipment before storing it. Follow the manufacturers' instructions and then thoroughly dry everything. Store it packed loosely, in a cool, dry place if possible. A solution of half a cup of Lysol in a gallon of water is effective yet mild enough to clean your gear and prevent mildew. Mildew causes serious deterioration of synthetic fabrics and in some cases will lead to delamination of the waterproof coatings. You can also use a weak bleach solution to wipe down equipment. Commercial mildew inhibitors can be very harsh; test strong cleaners on samples or small, noncritical corners before you commit to a full wiping down.

When coastal touring, take the time to paddle up a river and wash your clothes in fresh water. Salt in fabric attracts water and keeps clothing damp.

326 When doing laundry while camping, dissolve the soap in a large jar of water before putting it on the garments. Soap applied directly to clothes being washed with cold water does not distribute itself well and is hard to rinse off.

327 Rinse your laundry extra well. Soap left in the fabric promotes the buildup of objectionable odors.

328 When drying clothes near a fire, use a reflective emergency blanket behind them to concentrate the heat.

Fabric Repairs

To repair a rip in a tent, get the wrinkles out of the fabric by lightly ironing it on the outside around the tear. Use some clear tape on the outside to hold the tear together (1). On the inside of the fabric, frame the area to be repaired with masking tape (2). Carefully cut a patch of no-see-um netting to fit inside the masking tape frame, covering the tear (3). Place the netting into the frame and cover the entire patch with seam sealant, carefully incorporating

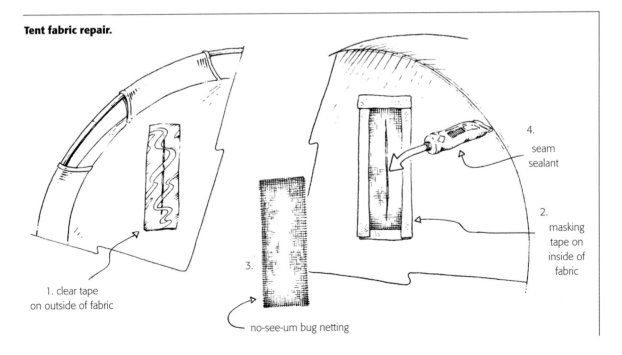

Tent fabric repair.

4. seam sealant

2. masking tape on inside of fabric

3.

1. clear tape on outside of fabric

no-see-um bug netting

the netting into the seal (4). A thin but thorough covering works best. Use a straight edge to smooth the sealant before it begins to set up. When the repair has completely dried, remove the tape from inside and outside. Your repair will look good, be waterproof, and last as long as the rest of the tent.

To repair torn fabric in the field, first baste the tear back together, then apply a piece of adhesive-backed fabric to the damaged area. It should have a good overlap onto the undamaged fabric. The patch will adhere properly only if the fabric is clean and warm. Press the patch firmly onto the fabric with a smooth round object.

329 Use a drop of seam sealant or neoprene glue to stop seams from unraveling.

330 Sailors have long carried a cloth roll called a *housewife* to hold needles, thread, buttons, a thimble, and patching material. On a piece of fabric 4 inches by 24 inches you can stitch pockets and elastic loops to hold items, and also spare buttons. You can include a needle threader, scissors, safety pins, and a piece of felt to hold needles. Sew ribbons on one end to tie the roll shut. Roll-up sewing kits waste far less space than boxes or jars.

Sailor's housewife.

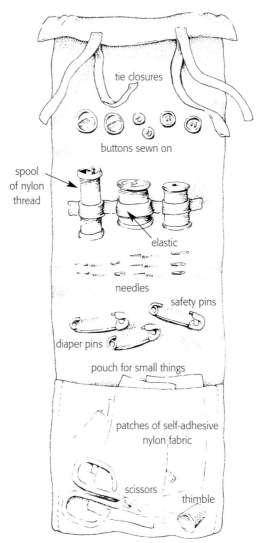

tie closures

buttons sewn on

spool of nylon thread

elastic

needles

safety pins

diaper pins

pouch for small things

patches of self-adhesive nylon fabric

scissors

thimble

Hypothermia: Staying Warm

When you're cold and wet you may experience hypothermia—the lowering of body temperature owing to heat loss. Body heat can be lost slowly through evaporation from wet clothes or through radiation when clothing is inadequate. As body temperature begins to drop, blood is diverted from the limbs to the body core. At first a victim will shiver vigorously and look pale. If the body continues to cool and circulation is further diverted, the lips and fingertips will turn bluish. Brain function will be diminished, leading to confusion and poor judgment. Dangerous levels of heat loss are evident when shivering becomes sporadic. Muscles grow increasingly rigid until shivering eventually stops. The mental state deteriorates from confusion to irrational behavior. Pulse and respiration slow, driving the body core into uncontrolled cooling.

Treating Hypothermia

The basic principles of rewarming a hypothermic victim are the same as for preventing hypothermia (see following). Avoid heat loss, supply food and water, and add external heat. Those suffering from mild hypothermia can be dried off, bundled up, and given a good snack and a warm drink. They have the capacity to rewarm themselves if heat loss is stopped and they are well nourished. Victims visibly disabled by heat loss need immediate intervention. They may not be able to make good decisions for themselves and are in danger of get-ting colder much faster. Sources of external heat such as heat packs or hot water bottles can be applied to armpits, groin, and neck. Severe hypothermia is a life-threatening condition that requires the intervention of a well-trained and well-equipped professional. Treatment that is incorrect or too aggressive can cause serious harm.

331 Take a wilderness first-aid course. It will cover the care and treatment of victims of hypothermia.

Preventing Hypothermia

Hypothermia is usually preventable. It's easier to stay warm than to get warm. Recognize the environmental conditions leading to hypothermia. Wear appropriate clothing for cold and wet conditions. Wear a hat at all times; a wet suit or dry suit with a hood to minimize heat loss is best. Wear polypropylene underwear to wick moisture away from the skin, fleece on top, and a windproof and waterproof outer layer.

332 Your mother had it right. Dress warmly, wear a hat, stay dry, and finish your lunch, including a glass of water.

333 Wearing layers lets a minimum of clothing meet a maximum of needs. Layers trap air to keep you warm and dry.

334 When you stop for a lunch break, pull on rain pants and a coat over your paddling clothes. Evaporation off the surface of a wet suit or paddling jacket will conduct heat out of your body very quickly.

335 When going ashore for a short time, leave your PFD on. It shields your ribcage, an area of significant heat loss.

336 Warm up before you leave a cold camp. Dress for paddling long before you depart. Pull on rain pants and jacket over your paddling clothes to trap a layer of insulating air.

337 If it's very cold, wear a microfleece or neoprene cold-water cap under your hat.

338 Wear pogies (gauntleted mittens that fit around the paddle shaft) seam side down so the water will drain out.

Pogies are neoprene or nylon hand warmers that fit over the paddle shaft.

Layering is an excellent way to stay warm. This paddler is wearing a polyester quick-dry hat, a dry suit made of breathable fabric, a wool sweater beneath, and fleece socks. He has sandals on to protect his feet from rocks or rough ground.

Camping in the Rain

Spending a lot of time and effort trying to stay dry can work against being comfortable in wet places. The most important thing in a wet campsite is a dry pair of socks.

339 If you have warm, dry feet, many hardships are easier to tolerate. Bring along synthetic socks that dry quickly. Keep a pair of synthetic waterproof-breathable socks to wear in wet shoes while ashore.

340 Bring along a wide-brimmed rain hat.

341 If you lack other rain gear, wear your neoprene paddling skullcap as a rain hat and a paddling jacket as a rain jacket.

342 Take off your rain pants and jacket when you're under the tarp. Even when you're out of the rain you'll get damp from within, since your perspiration can't evaporate buried beneath so many layers.

343 Keep one set of clothes dry at all times, even if you have to change into your damp clothes to fetch firewood or water. Being able to retreat into your tent and change into truly dry clothes is worth the effort.

344 Get wet. Take off all your clothes and stand in the rain. You may find it's your damp, stuffy clothes that are uncomfortable, not the rain.

Hyperthermia: Staying Cool

When a heat wave strikes, it takes several days for your body to acclimate to new demands. Take it easy at first and let your body adjust. Levels of hyperthermia vary from discomfort and nausea all the way up the scale to death. The good news is that prevention is easy and the basic treatment for all levels is the same. Keep cool, drink plenty of fluids, prevent sunburn, and keep your electrolytes balanced.

Treating Hyperthermia

Symptoms of hyperthermia generally treatable in the field are headache, nausea, dizziness, thirst, muscle cramps, and general weakness. Being overheated is one thing; a serious and debilitating case of heatstroke is quite another. Like severe hypothermia, severe hyperthermia is a life-threatening condition that requires advanced emergency care.

To treat hyperthermia, apply cold packs to armpits, groin, neck, and scalp. Evaporation from bare skin (in the shade) is more effective than wearing loose wet clothing. Repeatedly drink small quantities of dilute fluids and eat salty or sweet snacks to replace electrolytes. Take a complete rest.

Preventing Hyperthermia

345 Spend several days acclimating to a hot climate. Paddle a couple of hours in the morning and evening and rest in the shade in the middle of the day.

346 Drink a lot. Good hydration helps you keep cool. Sports drinks will help on two accounts: you're likely to drink significantly more of a flavored drink, and they contain electrolytes in the form of various salts that are essential for good hot-weather health. If you're drinking plain water, eat a little salted fruit or something similar.

347 Diluted drinks are metabolized better than salt pills or commercial electrolyte replacement drinks served full strength.

348 Keep cool; overheating is cumulative. Seek shade when ashore, and deliberately cool off if you start to overheat.

349 Check the color of your urine. Dark urine is a sign of dehydration; your urine should stay clear or light colored.

350 Prevent sunburn. A light shirt may not be enough coverage. A wet cotton T-shirt offers little protection; nylon is better. You can buy lightweight sun-protective garments rated to sun protection factor (SPF) 30. Wear a hat. Sunburn causes fluid loss and increases dehydration, aggravating hyperthermia, and it also increases the chances of melanoma.

351 Apply sunscreen generously both to exposed skin and beneath light cover-up clothing. Sun penetrates wet loose-weave clothing. Use a broad-spectrum waterproof sunscreen with an SPF of 30 or greater. Put it on thirty minutes before exposure and reapply frequently. Applying sunscreen to cool, dry skin makes the first layer last longer.

352 Use a lip balm with an SPF rating of 30.

Dressing for Paddling

Choosing clothing for comfortable paddling and possible rescue swimming takes thought. In temperate climates with cold water, you have to consider the hazards of an unanticipated swim. Any water below your body temperature will cool you down; the danger of hypothermia is particularly acute when you're immersed in even moderately cold water. It's not uncommon for paddlers to be forced out of their kayaks. If you're not prepared, the consequences can be unpleasant at best and tragic at worst. A dry suit is the most effective way to keep warm in the water. A 3 mm neoprene wet suit worn with a good-quality paddling jacket is more affordable and more flexible in its temperature range. In subtropical climates with warm water, shorts and a light dry top to fend off rain or sea spray may be sufficient.

Just hoping to stay dry in a marine environment is misguided faith. If you protect yourself from the water trying to get inside your clothes, you'll be a victim of the condensation inside trying to get out. It's best to judge your attire by how comfortable you are, not necessarily how dry. A jacket that leaves you a little hot and sweaty on a miserably cold, rainy, and windy day should be given high marks. Conversely, getting wet with a splash down your neck and arms on a warm, dry day may add to your comfort. The demands of practicing rolls and swimming rescues are very different from the comfort needs of a full day paddling to a campsite. As with most equipment purchases, a common theme repeats itself. The more compromises you make, the less effective the item will be. Also, a more specific design will often limit the garment's general utility. As always, layering garments helps provide a flexible wardrobe.

353 Buy the best dry suit or dry top you can afford. Dry tops have watertight neck and wrist seals. Paddling in the rain makes different demands on your clothing. You'll want to keep warm for a while, but after you've been paddling hard you'll want to vent some heat and still stay dry. Simple is better. Any unnecessary folds, pockets, tabs,

or straps are areas where leaks and damage can occur.

354 A single-tunnel, nonbreathable paddling jacket with adjustable neoprene wrist and neck closures will work well under a wide variety of conditions. It's less expensive than more technical dry tops. Some splash gets in, but it keeps out the rain. It can be worn as a rain top around camp.

355 Choose a paddling jacket that's too large rather than too small to minimize stress on the seams and maximize freedom of movement. An oversized paddling jacket can be pulled over a PFD. Stored within easy reach, it can be donned and doffed quickly and safely to suit the weather conditions.

356 Neoprene neck and wrist closures with Velcro are not watertight. Even when properly closed, they let in a small amount of water when you roll. They can be opened to permit considerable ventilation.

357 The warmth of a dry suit comes from two sources. The suit keeps the water out, and the layers of dry cloth worn underneath add warming insulation. Wear layers of quick-drying material to wick perspiration away from your body and trap air to keep you warm.

358 Dry suits can hold considerable air and provide too much buoyancy. Squeeze out most of the air before zipping up the suit.

359 For men, a dry suit with a waterproof crotch zipper installed costs more, but is very convenient.

360 A torn dry suit will take on a lot of water if the paddler comes out of the kayak and becomes a swimmer. It will quickly lose all buoyancy and maneuverability, and become quite hazardous. Always wear a PFD with your dry suit.

361 Waterproof-breathable fabrics must be clean and salt-free to work their best. Waterproof-breathable fabrics use body heat to push condensation out through the fabric. They're also much cooler to wear on a hot day. But salt and dirt infiltrating the weave not only will prevent evaporation of internal condensation but will draw external moisture through the fabric, leaving you very wet.

362 Latex wrist and neck seals should be protected. Keep your dry tops out of unnecessary sunlight. Ultraviolet protectants used for rubber products can be used to keep them supple. Seals that are layered inside the sleeves and neck of the garment will weather better than those exposed directly to the sun. Avoid getting sunscreen or other greasy substances on latex seals; the rubber will be degraded by the solvents and perfumes in many skin-care products.

363 After you buy a new dry suit or dry top with a watertight neck seal, wear it around the house for thirty minutes before you wear it paddling. It takes only a small amount of pressure in the right place to restrict blood flow through the arteries of the neck. Paddlers have passed out suddenly from wearing too snug a neck seal. Neck seals should be comfortable first and keep out water second.

364 Latex seals will loosen slightly after the first few wearings. If a neck seal is too snug it can be stretched slightly by pulling it over a water jug or some other neck-sized object. Be gentle, since seals will tear if handled too roughly. If the seal is still too tight, it can be resized by cutting it down a little, say ¼ to ½ inch.

365 Keep your hands warm. In a cold-water rescue, your fingers can quickly become disabled. Gloves or pogies can be an important safety item.

366 Wear footwear suitable for both swimming and walking on rugged ground. Rubber boots will have to be kicked off if you're in the water, then what happens when you have to scramble out on a rocky shore covered with barnacles? You may launch from a flat sandy beach but have to go ashore through the waves over rough ground.

367 Have a neoprene skullcap handy. Your head radiates a great deal of body heat and must be protected when you're in the water. Neoprene skullcaps and cold-water helmet liners are easy to carry.

368 To reduce odors in wet suit booties, wear synthetic sock liners. They help keep your booties clean and also make putting on wet booties early in the morning much more comfortable. They also wash and dry easily.

369 Keep your wet feet warm in cold water. Wet-suit booties never fit perfectly. Fleece or wool socks fill empty space and help keep your feet warmer. You can wash the socks and dry them much faster than you can dry your booties.

370 Take care of your feet. Wet and sweaty feet kept warm in neoprene booties or rubber boots are prone to athlete's foot, trench foot, and just plain getting real smelly. Keep your feet as dry as possible, and wash and dry them each evening.

CHAPTER 7

CAMPCRAFT

You'll spend more hours on shore in camp than at sea in the kayak. A comfortable camp will make your trip more pleasurable, and good camping skills will enhance your overall safety while touring. While you're ashore you need to replenish your energy reserves and get plenty of rest. This is most important in poor weather when sea conditions make extra demands on your skill and endurance. In marginal traveling conditions a comfortable camp will keep you safely ashore waiting for the storm to pass, whereas a cold, wet, and miserable one may prompt a bad decision and drive you out to sea.

Few circumstances permit sleeping in the open on the ground. In hot climates, cots keep you away from scorpions and other troublesome crawlers. A hammock can also get you up off the ground, and you can string a simple tarp above it as a rainfly. The modern two-piece tent and rainfly combination is the most versatile shelter for camping.

Tents

Camping out is a love-hate relationship. Some of my best, most memorable times have been spent stargazing on a moonless night well away from the lights and noise of civilization. On other memorable nights I've been wet, cold, and windswept in a tent that threatened to be blown away by a gale or washed away by a rising tide.

Tent Shapes

Bivvy sacks are enough shelter for some. Small and light, they're easy to pack. A bivvy sack under a tarp can be a secure shelter.

One-person bivouac tents often look like inflated bivvy sacks. Recommended for bicycle camping, these small tents have enough headroom so you can sit up in the doorway.

The simple A-frame pup tent is a classic favorite and comes in sizes big enough for three or four people. Its simple construction makes it fairly inexpensive. The rectangular floor layout makes good use of space, but the slanted walls

A blue rainfly over a white tent adds a friendly feel to a rocky campsite after a midnight rain squall in the Canadian arctic.

interfere with headroom. A-frame tents usually need to be staked down.

Dome tents with nearly circular floor plans have steep walls that maximize headroom and feel roomy. Dome tents are freestanding and don't have to be pegged down to maintain their shape. But they will need some staking to stay put. Even a moderate breeze can blow an empty dome tent down the beach.

Modern computer-designed tents mix the rectangular floor plan of A-frames with the hoop structure of a dome tent.

Tents for All Seasons

Tents rated as three-season tents will accommodate spring, summer, and fall in most latitudes. In a good campsite they'll be quite satisfactory for the occasional unanticipated bit of winter weather. But if you're planning regular winter or high-latitude camping you'll need a serious mountaineering specialty tent; get advice from an experienced guide. Three-season tents will usually be lighter, more compact, and easier to put up than four-season tents. Don't underestimate the need for plenty of mesh; good air circulation will minimize the considerable accumulation of moisture from condensation and breath vapor.

Four-season tents offer greater shelter and protection in windy, cold, and wet conditions. Made from more durable materials with greater reinforcement at stress points, these tents will be heavier. The design will use more interlocking poles and guyline attachment points, making them more complex to set up. The fly will extend closer to the ground to give greater coverage, but this will decrease air circulation. More technical adjustable wall vents may be included. A four-season tent will of course be more expensive than a three-season tent of the same quality.

Materials

The fabric used in most new tents is nylon taffeta or ripstop nylon; both are strong and lightweight. The floor material is often heavier, with a durable waterproof coating of polyurethane. Tent poles are most commonly lightweight aluminum or fiberglass strung together with shock cord for easy assembly.

Seams are the primary sites where water can enter your tent. Inspect the quality of the seam construction. Seams on the waterproof fly should be well lapped, and the best ones are also tape sealed on the inside. The point where the pole attachments are joined to the tent should be well sewn and possibly reinforced. A lot of tension is placed on the fabric loops that hold pegs and the ends of the poles. A well-designed and well-constructed tent will show even tension at all points of attachment. The corners in the floor should be well sewn and secure; uneven tension will cause leaks and early deterioration of seams. Zippers and vent openings must close well and operate smoothly.

The rainfly should give good coverage nearly to the ground, but a fly that comes down too far will restrict ventilation. The fly must not touch the main tent or water will migrate from one fabric to the other and into the tent. The fly should have attachment points for guylines to hold it away from the tent in windy conditions.

371 A tent that is quick and easy to erect is very desirable. Tents are often set up in the dark, in the rain, in the wind, and with waning patience. Practice setting up your tent at home several times. On the beach, with sand blowing in your eyes and mosquitoes nibbling at your nose, you'll want to get your tent up quickly with no unnecessary fuss.

372 Before you buy a tent, climb inside it. Sit around, invite in a friend, and bring in a couple of dry bags full of gear. Could you comfortably change your clothes in there? Can you get in and out the door without crawling?

373 Dark-colored fabric makes the tent's interior dark and absorbs more harmful ultraviolet light, which causes the material to deteriorate. White, gold, teal, and blue are popular colors. They don't clash with the natural surroundings, and the interior light is bright and cheery. In hot climates, light colors keep the interior cooler.

374 Seal the seams of your tent. Manufacturers of even the most expensive tents with taped seams recommend sealing seams to prevent the needle holes from leaking. Seam sealant is sold in tubes and bottles and is best applied to the uncoated side of the fabric.

375 Two thin applications are usually necessary for thorough waterproofing. You may want to seal the seams once each camping season.

376 Use a plastic syringe (available in drugstores) to apply seam sealant to sewn seams; you'll have more control and do a neater job.

377 Dry your tent thoroughly before storing it. Storing your tent wet will cause the fabric to delaminate and the

Flying pup tent.

A FLYING PUP TENT

During many trips along the British Columbia rain coast, I camped with only a canvas navy hammock instead of a tent. Strung tightly between two trees above rocky or wet ground, with a nylon fly clothespinned to a line overhead, the hammock kept me off the ground, dry and cozy. It looked like a flying pup tent. On warm, sunny afternoons and moonlight evenings a hammock beats a tent every time.

coating to peel off. Drying out your tent will also prevent mildew, which smells bad and makes the fabric deteriorate. (See pages 75-76) on preventing mildew and washing fabrics.)

378 Always assemble and disassemble your tent poles carefully. Simply shaking them out of the bag can cause minor nicks and bends that make the poles more difficult to thread into the tent and can damage the fabric.

379 Keep your tent door closed to keep the bugs out. Before you collapse your tent, zip the door shut. If your next campsite is buggy, they won't get in before you do.

380 Sleep in a tent. Bears, snakes, and spiders will usually check out the tent without bothering the occupant.

381 If it's hot and dry, remove your tent fly to increase ventilation and improve the view.

382 Keep your tent out of direct sunlight. Although this may seem silly or impossible, ultraviolet light is a prime factor in the deterioration of synthetic fabric. Try to pitch your tent in the shade or put it up late in the day. You might simply pull out your interior groundsheet and drape it over the tent in the heat of the day.

383 If you use a groundsheet under the tent, make sure it's smaller than the outline of the floor or you'll be sleeping in a puddle. As the rain runs down the side of the tent, it should fall onto the ground and drain away from the tent, not onto the groundsheet. Water flowing across the ground can also run under the tent and onto the groundsheet.

384 Use a piece of inexpensive clear plastic sheeting from a building supply store as a second groundsheet inside the tent and wrap it a few inches up the wall, it will keep you dry even if the floor does leak.

385 Take along an extra piece of clear plastic sheeting 8 feet by 12. Folded up, it takes virtually no space. Use it as an emergency tarp, cover your dry firewood, or drape it over your tent in a downpour.

386 In colder climates you can use a Mylar emergency blanket as a groundsheet inside your tent. With the reflective side up, it will add insulation.

387 Take along several extra tent stakes. Stakes of nonbending metal are worth the extra expense. Plastic pegs are larger and sometimes difficult to pound into rocky ground.

388 Thoroughly rinse the ends of your tent poles. Salt from beach sand gets into their hollow ends and corrodes the aluminum plugs so they swell and split the shafts.

389 Take along an extra tent pole sleeve and ferrule for repairs.

390 To improvise a repair on a broken tent pole, cut off the ends of an aluminum can and slice the cylinder open. Wrap the aluminum around the broken pole a couple of times, then bind the repair with whipping twine or several layers of nylon strapping tape.

Sleeping Bags

Ask campers what they most desperately want to keep dry and they'll say it's their sleeping bags. Dry socks and a dry sleeping bag offer rest and comfort. For a hypothermic or sick camper, a warm, dry sleeping bag can be critical. When traveling by kayak it's a constant challenge to keep your sleeping bag dry. In a tent, moisture from your breath saturates the air and perspiration dampens the bag from the inside. A sleeping bag should dry easily, and if it can't be dried, the wet bag should still provide enough insulation to keep you warm.

391 Buy a sleeping bag filled with synthetic fibers. They dry more easily than goose down and retain their insulation value better when wet.

392 Silk sleeping bag liners are dry and comfy. A liner adds warmth and cleanliness, and silk is easy to wash and dry.

393 Double-bag your sleeping bag by putting a large plastic bag inside its nylon stuff sack. Squeeze the air out of the plastic bag, twist it closed, then close the stuff sack. The nylon stuff sack will protect the plastic, and the plastic will protect the sleeping bag.

394 Buy a lightweight bag and an overbag to create a sleeping system. An overbag can add as much as twenty degrees Fahrenheit to the bag's temperature rating. If one layer gets wet, the other might still be dry. Two light bags pack more easily than one heavy one. For subtropical camping the light bag or just the overbag would be enough.

395 Use a sleeping pad. There's substantial heat loss to the ground when you sleep without one, and besides warmth a sleeping pad adds considerable comfort. Therm-a-Rest pads deflate and pack well into the ends of a kayak. Closed-cell foam pads take up considerably more space.

Setting Up Camp

A campsite chosen on a good day should also keep you comfortable on a bad day. Choose a landing site that will permit a safe launch the next day. A small, secluded beach facing the open water with a promise of great sunsets or sunrises may be swept with dangerous surf in the morning. When you pick a campsite you need to consider the profile of the beach, since you'll have to

CAMPING ON A LEE SHORE

Late in June, it was a wonderful sunny, calm day on the open coast. As I approached a tiny enclosed beach, white sand glistened next to clear blue water, adding to the tropical effect of the afternoon sun on my back. My private beach was sheltered from the low swell by high rock cliffs and a house-sized rock in the center, with a narrow entry on each side. Clearing a space high among the driftwood logs, I pitched my tent and made dinner using a large wooden spool as a table. I thought it was paradise.

In the morning torrential rain, driven by a full gale, came in my open tent door. My once sublime campground was now a trap. As the tide rose higher with the extra pull at the summer solstice, the incoming surf threatened to lift all the driftwood into a seething, dangerous mass. There was no possibility of navigating the narrow passage out to the open water. Half panicked, I had to drag my tent, my kayak, and all my gear into the dense, rain-drenched forest behind the beach. I quickly was soaked, scared, and seriously chilled. Without a tent site and with too much wind to set up even a simple tarp, it took some time for me to realize that I had to take control of the situation—to make a shelter, a fire, and a meal and find some dry clothes. A day later the storm came to an end. It had taken both stormy days for me to reestablish comfortable living arrangements out of the chaos. When I left I found that only half a mile away around the corner there was a bay with a small beach completely sheltered from the open water. My quick, unconsidered choice of a campsite cost me two uncomfortable and anxious days.

both land and launch there. Time your landings and launchings to coincide with high tide. If you land on a flat sandy beach during an evening high tide, in the morning you may find yourself on a fringe of sand above a hundred yards of rough rock. Keep your tent and your kayak as close together as possible. Every bit of gear you need is in your kayak, and each time you make and break camp there will be many trips back and forth. Steeper beaches make for shorter trips to and from the shoreline, but try to camp on beaches with a reasonable slope. Beware of rough dumping surf on steep beaches.

396 Consider the effect passing ships will have on your campsite. The waves they produce can run a long way up a shelving beach. Camera gear I once left on the rocky shore was washed into the sea. Fortunately, since it was submersible, I recovered it unharmed.

397 Bring a small electronic travel clock (they don't tick!). Setting an alarm clock when you're out paddling may seem a bit harsh, but you may need to check the late-night high tide rising on your campsite or wake up for an early morning departure.

398 You can't beat a good tarp. They keep you dry in the rain and shaded in the sun. Your tarp should be the first element of your campsite to be raised and the last to come down. Catenary-cut nylon tarps are easy to put up; they stay up in the wind without flapping and shed water instead of building up small lakes to cascade onto your head at the worst possible time. After the tarp is up you can start to unload other gear and make camp. Pitching your tent under a tarp can make living in the rain for three days seem quite reasonable.

399 Use a small nylon bag to hold a collection of light lines of various lengths. When you're setting up tarps and tents, an extra line is always useful. Pieces of ⅛-inch nylon line 10 to 20 feet long work well.

Tents provide shelter during a gale.

Catenary tarp over a tent. The catenary cut is curved under tension to increase its shedding of wind and rain.

Campfires

Open campfires are coming under serious criticism. Beaches become scarred and dirty with their remains. Keep campfires small, and build them where they'll damage the land as little as possible. If a fire pit already exists, should you use it? One choice is to dismantle it and return the site to a more natural state. Using the already sooty mound is another choice. Cleaning it up before you leave or leaving it for another camper are other options. Each situation is different.

400 Beware of the fire pit that's been used as a garbage incinerator. Partially burned food waste is just overcooked treats that will attract wildlife.

401 In rainy weather, carry along some kindling. Use today's fire to dry out tomorrow's kindling. A few sticks take up little room in your kayak, and a small fire can be a big comfort.

402 Cotton balls saturated with Vaseline make excellent fire starters. Keep several in a film canister sealed with tape or in a Ziploc bag.

403 Beeswax burns much hotter than paraffin. Fire starters that use beeswax are the most effective.

404 Scouts and Guides use buddy burners as emergency stoves or fire starters. (See pages 66–67) for how to make one.)

405 Bring a saw to cut firewood. Lightweight pruning saws with locking blades fold to fit into pockets or tool belts. The teeth are designed to cut live wood, so they also work well on the wet driftwood often found around campsites. (See photo, page 93.)

Avoiding Bears

Do Not Feed the Bears! Do not feed bears inadvertently while you're in camp or after you leave. There are wilderness campsites that are no longer safe for kayak camping because the bears are accustomed to feeding on leftovers.

406 Leave a clean campsite for the next paddler, with no evidence of your visit.

407 Think about bears when you plan your provisions and your menus. Meat and fish are super bear attractants, but bears are omnivores and have a passion for berries as well. Freeze-dried foods have very little odor. Canned goods have no odor but will add a lot of weight to your load.

408 Avoidance is the very best tactic when dealing with bears. Bears that live near dirty, frequently used campsites are unpredictable and dangerous.

Garden pruning saw.

EGG CARTON FIRE STARTERS

Lighting a fire with damp driftwood can be difficult. Something light to carry and easy to ignite will make fire starting much easier. Here's one way to make fire starters from items around the house. You'll need:

- the bottom of an empty cardboard egg carton
- enough dryer lint to fill the carton
- 24 inches of cotton string
- approx. ¼ cup melted wax (use broken candles or paraffin from jam jars)

Fill the spaces in the egg carton with the dryer lint. Cut twelve lengths of the string, each about half an inch long. Put one piece of string in each lint-filled hollow, making sure it sticks straight up. Melt the candle wax or paraffin in a tin can floating in a saucepan half full of water over a hot burner. The water will keep the wax from overheating and igniting. When the wax is liquid, pour it over the lint and let it cool.

In camp, tear off one of your fire starters and put it at the bottom of your unlit fire. They're a little bulky, but they'll burn long enough to let you dry some tinder and move to larger fuel.

In fact, it is the campsite itself that is dangerous and inconsiderate previous campers that make it so. Bears that have become familiar with garbage dumps are infinitely more hazardous than bears that have had little or no contact with people and their leftovers. When choosing a campsite, consider whether it's frequently used by campers and whether there's a village or industrial camp nearby that may leave garbage out.

409 Remove all food and food-related items from your kayak. A bear's sense of smell is better than a dog's. Trying to hide food from a hungry bear by wrapping your cheese tightly in sandwich wrap and putting it in a plastic container in your aft hatch is pretty much useless.

410 You want the bears to know you're there. Wild animals will try to avoid you. Camp on the upwind end of the beach so bears will smell you long before you know they're near. Drinks lots of fluids and spread your scent around.

411 Remember, bears are good swimmers! Small islets offshore are less likely to be home to bears, but the smell of fresh-cooked fish or other delicacies just might bring them out, and you will have nowhere to run!

412 If a bear cub is coming your way, it's probably not curious; it more likely is going back to its mother. Get out of there!

413 If confronted by a bear, look big and talk firm and low. Don't make eye contact and it will probably go away. Bears don't see well at all, and when you're downwind the bear will not smell you. If you make your presence known, it should run away. A bear that keeps coming in spite of your presence is probably familiar with camp food and won't go away. You'll have to leave.

414 Check the area for signs of well-traveled trails. When selecting a tent site on the beach, be sure your tent isn't blocking a path leading into the woods. Often paths that bears use frequently are obscured by lush greenery stimulated by the sun at the edge of the beach. Just a couple of feet inside the forest the path opens up.

415 Keep some kind of noisemaker in your tent. Airhorns provide enough noise to scare off most animals.

416 Pepper spray canisters explicitly for deterring bears are available. However, local laws may restrict the purchase and use of pepper spray.

417 In areas where grizzly or polar bears may be found, bear bangers should be carried while on land. Bear bangers come with a pen-size handheld launcher and shoot a small explosive noisemaker about 30 yards.

418 Select your campsite with good sight lines and escape routes—for both campers and wildlife. You should be able to see one another, and both should have unrestricted exits.

419 Use one campsite for eating dinner and another for sleeping. After dinner you can paddle for an hour and choose a "clean" site for your tents. If you're

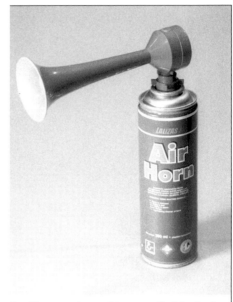

An airhorn can be used to scare off wild animals.

not going to paddle away after dinner, your kitchen should be a hundred yards downwind from your sleeping site. A kitchen located so that it will be washed over by the next high tide is best.

420 Measure food portions carefully. Disposing of leftovers is a sure way to attract animals. Simply tossing them into the outgoing tide is not enough. The returning tide has a nasty habit of returning your garbage.

421 Check the nearby woods for berries. As the season progresses, bears follow the ripening berries. Though they may not have been foraging on your beach last week, they may visit soon if a new species has become ripe.

422 Wear a cotton apron or long shirt while cooking to keep food debris off your clothes. It can be washed, and you can store it in a bearproof container or hang it up with your food.

KEEP THE PATH CLEAR

Very early one morning I was awakened by a question. Three of us had paddled to a remote pea-gravel beach and had set up our tents high on the narrow beach next to the dense forest undergrowth. "Is that you?" a voice asked. Someone must have been up walking on the beach, because the very next thing I heard was footsteps in the gravel inches from my head. My thoughts quickened enough to put together the pieces of the puzzle. Automatically I clapped my hands loudly and shouted, "HEY! HEY! HEY!"

The next sound was gravel hitting my tent and a great rustling crash as a bear bolted into the woods. When I got up to look at the beach, it was obvious what had happened. Right behind my tent, obscured by lush foliage, was a well-traveled path. The only access to it was across the corner of my tent.

423 If you catch fish, take the remains well offshore where the tide will carry them away and not return them to your beach.

424 Hang your food 15 feet high and 9 feet out from the trunk of a tree. Also hang up cosmetics or any other items with strong odors.

425 Line used to raise food bags should not be stretchy. Parachute cord works well. Nylon line stretches so much that hoisting a heavy bag is nearly impossible.

426 Before you hang your food, rig a pulley—a carabiner will do. Raising a heavy bag with a line draped over a rough branch takes a lot of pulling on a thin line with tender hands. First tie a rock to one end of a line and a carabiner to the other. Throw the rock over the branch. (If the rock gets hung up in the tree you'll lose the rock, not the carabiner. Bring a small bag to hold the rock; tying the bag onto your line is much easier than tying on a rock.) Thread your food bag line through the carabiner and raise the carabiner up to the branch, then tie off the carabiner line. Raise your food bag with the line running through the carabiner.

CORNERED

It's often true that surf landings are gentler at the ends of the beach. One day, landing in just such a spot, we set up camp sheltered from the gale-force wind and torrential rain by an adjacent steep cliff. It was a lovely little site that included a trickling stream of fresh water. The next day, while we were waiting out the gale, a large male bear began foraging on the beach. We watched him amble toward us, closing several hundred yards. Our loud conversation and pointed, uncomplimentary comments didn't deter this local resident. The strong onshore wind kept our scent away, and surf dumping noisily onto the gravel beach made hearing difficult. As he approached within a stone's throw, we realized we were trapped against the cliffs at the end of the beach. When he got really close our energetic clanging of pots and pans finally caught his attention and he scrambled off into the woods.

Hanging a food bag from a tree. Note the carabiner used as a pulley.

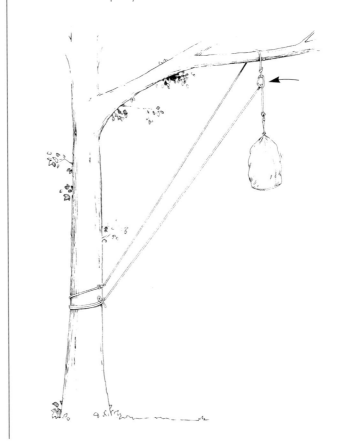

Staying Comfortable in Wind and Rain

Windy and rainy days in camp can put the most resilient of us into a mind-numbing stupor followed by a right bad mood. This is as much the result of a lack of planning as of the weather. There are many things you can do when trapped ashore. Save some tasks especially for the nonpaddling days.

427 Don't sulk about the weather, go anyway. Just get out and do something—it will pick up your mood. It's the sitting around that's mind numbing, not the rain.

428 Go out paddling on rainy days. The hard part is getting into damp, cold paddling gear, but once you're in the kayak you'll warm up and forget the rain. Those left back in camp will wish they'd gone out.

429 Go for a swim. Rainy days are the time to wash; look forward to foul weather as a chance to clean up and get a good freshwater rinse.

430 Do the wash. Hot, sunny days without an abundance of fresh water quickly leave synthetic clothes stinky. Clothes washed and hung out to rinse in the rain will dry quickly when the time is right.

431 Bring some toys. Games, cards, a Hacky Sack, a book of brain teasers, crossword puzzles, or tarot cards will entertain you for hours.

432 Play "Two Truths and a Lie." Everybody makes three statements; two must be true and the other must be a lie. The object is to discern the lie. It's a good way to get to know your fellow paddlers.

433 Take some pictures. Photos taken in the rain can show rich, well-saturated colors because the lighting is very even, without excessive contrast. A rainy-day picture of a colorful subject can be a thing of beauty.

SHOWER WITH A FRIEND

On the third day camped on a rainy coast, my buddy of Finnish descent reminisced about soaking in a hot sauna, then running out into cold water or snow, followed by more heat and flailing yourself with bay branches. Misery is the mother of invention–here's the rain coast version of the Finnish tradition.

First, make a beach fire. Second, get naked or as naked as modesty permits. Third, run screaming into the cold ocean water, soap up (with biodegradable soap), and wash thoroughly. Return to the fire with a viscose towel in hand. Standing close to the fire will keep you warm on one side; you can rub the other side with the towel.

We soon found that showering in the rain was preferable to standing around in layers of warm clothing and clammy rain gear. "Showers" began to last a very long time, and we looked forward to them with great anticipation. A new rain coast custom had been born.

CHAPTER 8

TRIP PLANNING

*T*he pleasure of getting outdoors and paddling away from the beach can turn sour if you fail to anticipate the unexpected. As paddlers gain skill and self-confidence they explore new limits, searching for challenges. Novices often have a low threshold for perceived risk and make conservative choices. A more experienced paddler will perceive less risk and take greater chances. As the paddling environment you choose becomes more dynamic and complex, a growing number of smaller risks can compound to overwhelming proportions.

ASK A SIMPLE QUESTION

In the middle of a long trip I made a VHF radiotelephone call home to say I was getting along fine. Though I could hear my wife's voice very clearly, her reception of my transmission was so poor that any communication beyond a simple yes or no was impossible. The call caused confusion and worry. A couple of days later I made a second call with much better results. This episode taught both of us a simple lesson. When radio reception is bad, ask questions that can be answered simply. To be clearly understood, repeat your answer. "Are you on schedule?" Respond, "Yes, yes, yes." With a detailed float plan filed, this answer gives your location and information about your general rate of progress.

FLOAT PLAN

Leave your float plan at home with a levelheaded and decisive person, preferably one who clearly understands where you'll be paddling and the conditions you'll encounter. That person needs to know whether you're likely to forge out into bad weather or to make a secure camp and stay ashore. Carry another copy of the plan in your kayak.

Name: _____

Date: _____

Address: _____

Home phone number: _____

Work phone number: _____

Car make and color: _____

Car license number: _____

Emergency contact's name and telephone number: _____

Medical conditions: _____

Doctor's name and telephone number: _____

Launch site: _____

Launch time: _____

Destination: _____

Arrival time: _____

Return date and time: _____

Call for search if not back by: [date and time] _____

Number of people in group: _____

Leader's name: _____

Type and color of kayak(s): _____

VHF radio call sign: _____

Cell phone number: _____

Radio contact times: _____

Emergency equipment carried: _____

Survival equipment carried: _____

Know your limits and expand them one at a time. Your first overnight trip paddling a fully loaded kayak should be in comfortable sea conditions with a good weather forecast. You should learn surf landings and breakouts with an instructor at a gently sloping sand beach. Wilderness camping is a skill of its own, greatly enhanced by the experience of a well-guided trip. With proper preparation, when the day comes for you to take your kayak ten days from the nearest phone and outrun a gale by surfing through 6-foot breakers into a wilderness campsite visited by bears, you just might have fun rather than succumbing to an anxiety-driven adrenaline overdose.

Each trip should have a purpose. Having a goal helps in decision making and safety management. If you're taking a friend out for a first overnight kayaking trip, stick to crossing only short stretches of open water. Advanced training in wind and waves should be conducted where safe landings sites are frequent.

434 If you make last-minute changes of plans, record them on the copy of your float plan you carry in your kayak and inform the recipient of the original plan.

435 Float plans left in vehicles tell thieves how long you'll be away and whose home might be vacant.

436 If you're overdue on your float plan, call the recipient of your plan or the appropriate authorities.

437 Factor extra time into your float plan so that a short delay or minor change of plans doesn't cause undue concern and initiate an unnecessary search and rescue.

The holder of your float plan must have an answering machine or voice mail so that all calls are answered. Collect calls won't work, so have a way to pay for any calls. Ask for privacy before reading credit card numbers or radiotelephone account numbers over the radio. The operator will jam your signal so eavesdroppers will hear only a steady beep. Alternatively, you can register your number with the marine operator in advance.

NO ANSWER

In mountainous fjord areas radio reception is available infrequently. I thought I had planned wisely to make a radiotelephone call when I was in one of the few locations where a radio tower was within range of my handheld VHF unit. It would be four or five days' travel to the next location that promised any radio transmission at all, and I felt it was important to make a call that day. The transmission was good, but the phone rang unanswered. I had an alternative number to call, but it too rang without an answer. Fortunately my float plan was not specific about when I would call home; I knew transmission on my end was going to be difficult, so nobody was alarmed by not receiving a call. However, I was troubled for days about not getting that call out. A few days later someone was home, and the news of my progress was clearly received.

Transportation

Before you and your partner start paddling, you'll have to transport your kayaks, probably on a cartop rack. Roof transportation is the most hazardous environment for your kayak.

Buy a good roof rack and the means to securely tie down a kayak or two. The rack will pay for itself by keeping your valuable boat in one piece. Add good-quality kayak cradles with nylon straps and locking metal buckles—they provide the best support and the easiest way to load and unload. Cradles or shaped foam blocks with wide surfaces support the hull and prevent deformations caused by strapping the kayak down improperly.

438 Completely empty your kayak before loading it onto your roof rack. A quick stop puts considerable strain both on a loaded kayak and on your roof rack.

439 Space the crossbars of your roof rack as far apart as possible. Sideways forces on long sea kayaks can be sudden and very strong. A passing tractor trailer or a strong gust of wind can exert considerable twisting force.

440 Place your roof rack as far to the back as you can. For loading a kayak onto a very tall camper or van, have a rack custom-installed at the extreme back edge of the roof where it's easier to reach.

441 Always use bow and stern tie-downs. If one rack crossbar, a saddle, or one tie-down line fails, your kayak can be airborne—and it's not equipped with landing gear.

Strapping the rudder in position during transport.

bungee for holding down rudder

442 Always tie down your kayak yourself. If your new kayak flies off the roof rack, have no one but yourself to blame.

443 Tie the kayak down first, chat later. Always tie your kayak onto the roof rack before you walk away or do any other chores. It's easy to forget to do it later.

444 Secure your kayak's bow line. If the line drops to the ground it will be run over, pulling the kayak down over the car windshield and causing heavy damage.

445 Use only one set of kayak rollers. One set of rollers on the back roof rack crossbar and a saddle on the front bar make for easy loading and secure traveling. Two sets of rollers can launch a kayak onto the car hood or the road; exchanging the front rollers for a saddle offers some friction. One set is still convenient.

446 Use a cockpit cover to keep the rain out. In a hard rain considerable water can collect inside the kayak, and if you have to brake hard, damage can occur as the water moves forward.

447 Strap your rudder securely in the raised position. A rudder dancing freely in the wind will get damaged.

448 Hang a flag from the rudder. Paddlers loading and unloading trunks and hatchbacks are apt to hit their heads on hard metal rudder assemblies, and head lacerations often need stitches. Highway laws may also require that protruding sterns be flagged. Some jurisdictions may require a red light at night. Check with local police.

449 Attach a tennis ball to your roof

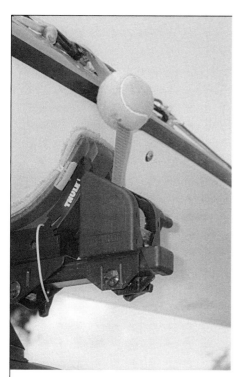

Tennis ball used to carry a roof-rack strap over the top of the load.

rack straps. Cut a 1-inch slot with a utility knife on one side of the ball; on the opposite side, cut another slot at a 90-degree angle to the first one. Slide the 1-inch webbing strap through the tennis ball. The strapping will take a quarter turn inside the ball because the slots are cut at different angles. When you toss the strap over the kayak on the roof rack, the ball will carry it across. Having the twist inside stops the ball from sliding off the end. Push the ball back up the strap when you fasten the buckle.

450 Straps fastened with metal buckles should also be secured with a half hitch at the ends. Buckles get stiff, and springs weaken over time. One faulty buckle can cause a catastrophic loss.

451 A kayak should be loaded onto the roof rack with the keel down. Keels are built stronger than decks and will take the load better. Try to place your kayak so that flat areas of the hull rest on the rack.

452 Use saddles or shaped padding on roof racks to help distribute the considerable load placed on the hull. Plastics, including fiberglass, do not hold up well when pressure is concentrated on a small area.

453 For economical or temporary padding on a roof rack use a Pool Noodle, a long foam water toy. Slice off two pieces the width of the rack and cut slots in the bottoms so they fit securely over the crossbars. On the top side carve out hollows to approximately fit your kayak's hull. Fasten the foam pieces to the roof rack with "zap straps" (skinny nylon sliding-locking ties).

454 If you have to transport a kayak without a roof rack, you can make cradles from two blocks of rigid foam and nylon webbing. Carve out a saddle in a rectangular block of Minicel foam. Minicel foam cuts easily with a hacksaw or serrated knife. Pierce the block to receive a length of 1-inch nylon webbing. Glue a piece of nonskid material to the bottom of the block. The webbing can be wrapped around the roof and through the doors and buckled inside the car.

455 From the side, load one end of your kayak onto the rack before lifting the other end. To make single-handed loading onto an awkward roof rack easier, extend the rack out to the side with some rigid tubing slipped over the end of the crossbar or inserted into it. First lift the bow and rest it on the extension,

An improvised kayak cradle. Cut 3-inch-wide lengths of closed-cell foam from an inexpensive sleeping pad and roll them to form cylinders. Wrap the foam rolls to the roof rack with clear packing tape.

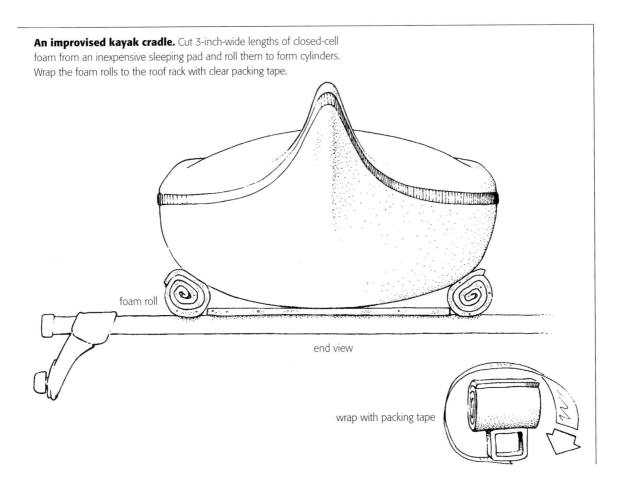

foam roll

end view

wrap with packing tape

Loading a kayak from the side of the car.

then lift the stern. (See top photo, page 103.)

456 Use an inexpensive plastic step stool to reach the top of tall vehicles. We know you can do without it, but your back will thank you.

457 Use ⅜-inch polyester line to tie a kayak onto a roof rack or for bow and stern tie-downs. Nylon line has considerable stretch and will "grow" when wet; thinner line may be strong enough, but heavier line is easier to tie and untie.

458 Use a trucker's hitch to fasten rope tie-downs (see page 123); it will let you control the tension on the line. Too much rope pressure, especially without a saddle to distribute the load, can damage the hull.

459 Cinch your tie-downs. The vertical load they place on the kayak can deform the hull. A final circling of the tie-downs adds some horizontal pressure and creates a more secure fastening. (See illustration and photo below.)

460 To let the kayak slide along the back saddle, glue carpet on the pads. There will be plenty of friction from the front saddle to stop the kayak from moving when it's finally tied down.

461 Protect your vehicle with a rubber-backed bath mat. Place the mat over the end of the roof with the nonskid surface down. Your kayak will slide but the mat won't. You can also stand on the mat when you change clothes.

462 Lock your kayak onto your roof rack. There are several security cable systems for kayaks. An automotive steering-wheel lock like the Club across the cockpit coaming is a theft deterrent and is also a strong place to fasten security cables.

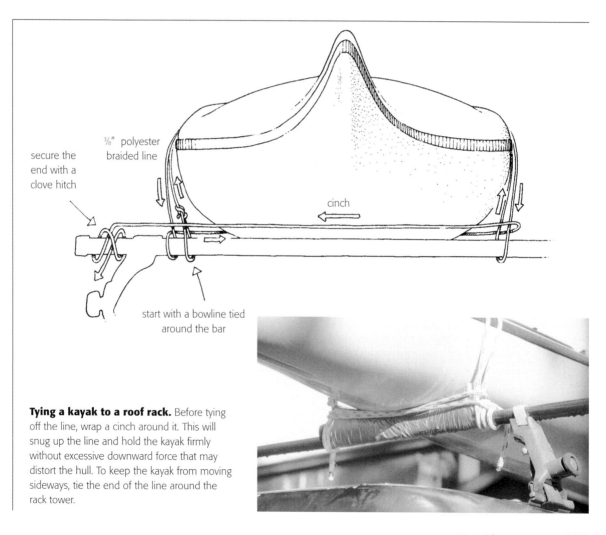

secure the end with a clove hitch

⅜" polyester braided line

cinch

start with a bowline tied around the bar

Tying a kayak to a roof rack. Before tying off the line, wrap a cinch around it. This will snug up the line and hold the kayak firmly without excessive downward force that may distort the hull. To keep the kayak from moving sideways, tie the end of the line around the rack tower.

Locking a kayak on a roof rack using a steering-wheel lock and a cable.

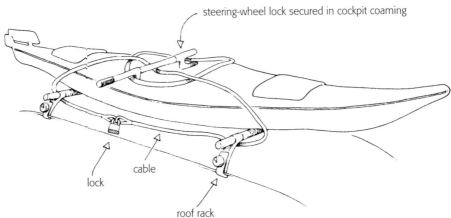

steering-wheel lock secured in cockpit coaming

cable

lock

roof rack

463 Leave your car completely empty, with no items visible to invite thieves. **464** Check your car or homeowner's insurance policy. You may not be covered if your kayak flies off the roof rack or is stolen. The most common cause of major damage is for the kayak to lose its grip on the roof rack and come free while you're driving. Remember to inquire about the contents as well. Your VHF radio and deck compass might be in your kayak when it falls off the roof rack.

Risk Assessment

Judging the overall hazard of a trip or a single day's paddling means assessing the number and severity of risks you'll encounter. Wind is a risk factor; how much wind you're willing to take is a judgment call.

When planning a trip, make a list of the various risks and note how severe each one is. One very large risk could be overwhelming, or many small risks might add up to an unacceptable level. Work to limit both the number of risks and the severity of each.

During your trip keep a mental note of how many small things change or don't go quite right. After a plan has been formulated and the kayaks have left the beach, risk assessment needs to continue. Small problems or changes in conditions are red flags that signal an increase in the present risk. Dangerous incidents are most often preceded by a series of seemingly inconsequential red flags. The sum of small increases in risk can subtly build to dramatic proportions and tragic consequences.

The list below presents seven risk factors: self-reliance, experience, judgment, skill, weather, sea state, and temperature. Each risk could be scored as mild (1) to severe (5). Score your trip on each of the scales (below) and determine the total. Consider how you could eliminate or reduce a risk. Add items to the checklist as you need to.

Beginners must realize they may lack the knowledge or experience to accurately assess the risks they'll face. They should seek the advice of well-respected, experienced paddlers.

Seasoned paddlers must temper bravado with humility. Taking on too many risks, then encountering an unexpected increase in their severity such as changes in local weather, can turn an adventure into a calamity.

Once you know the sum you have an overall estimate of the potential risk. You can make trip plans to decrease the number and severity of risk factors. Plans also need to accommodate changing circumstances en route. If a member of the group develops increasing soreness in a shoulder, you may need to substitute a shorter day and a different campsite.

465 Speak out to your paddling partners about the risks as you perceive them. Voice your concerns and know your personal limits. If you don't think it's safe, then it probably is not safe for you. Acknowledging changing circumstances should stimulate a reassessment of the total risk potential and possibly a change of plans.

466 Make well-considered plans. Assess the skills of individual members in the group and plan trips to accommodate the skill level of the weakest paddler.

467 Eliminate the risk altogether. You can choose to change course to avoid a windy open-water crossing. Communicate changes to the members of the

KAYAKING RISK FACTORS

Rated from mild (1) to severe (5)

Self-Reliance						
supervised, sheltered water	1	2	3	4	5	solo, open-water crossing
Experience						
well-trained, experienced kayaker	1	2	3	4	5	first-time kayaker
Judgment						
aware and prudent	1	2	3	4	5	unaware and reckless
Skill						
surf landings	1	2	3	4	5	wet exit and swim
Weather						
calm wind, stable forecast	1	2	3	4	5	stiff breeze, deteriorating weather
Sea State						
calm sea, no current	1	2	3	4	5	breaking waves, 3-knot current
Temperature						
tropics 80°F	1	2	3	4	5	arctic 32°F

group and to the recipient of your float plan.

468 Have the right equipment. You can moderate the risk of cold water immersion by wearing a dry suit.

469 Have good skills. Learning to roll makes a capsize less likely and lessens the consequences if one does occur.

470 Be prepared. Take a wilderness first-aid course before heading out to the boonies.

471 Remain alert to changes in environmental conditions and the health of your party.

Environmental Impact of Kayakers

Before sea kayaks became popular, many remote shores were seldom visited. Now more and more ecotourists, including self-supported sea kayakers, are congregating in the last of the unsullied natural places. It's easy to think of a kayak's quiet, human-powered mode as one of benign simplicity. But even its quiet, seaworthy nature creates an environmental impact. Approach a raucous sea lion colony, and the stampede to the water may trample some of this year's pups. Seabirds nesting on cliffs will fly off the nest, exposing their eggs to predators. Sea otter moms keep their young on their chests and diligently dry them off to keep them warm. While you stay warm and dry in your kayak, your close approach means the baby otter takes a cold bath.

In busy coastal campsites, bears get used to food left behind by careless campers. The now well-trained bear will seek out an easy meal in every available campsite and may eventually be killed by park managers. The long-term effect of such encounters has been to diminish the experience of all who follow. Fortunately, the point of view is changing in favor of wildlife. In some parks bearproof containers are mandatory. Camping may be permitted only where aboveground food caches have been built.

The pressure on our ecosystems continues to grow as human activity expands. Sea kayakers can learn to be part of an ecosystem, acting as equals with its other inhabitants. If they don't, there will be an irreversible decline of the touring experience. We can choose to find a niche where we can observe without interfering. Educating ourselves is increasingly important.

472 During your stay leave out nothing to attract wildlife. Live in a clean camp-

BALD EAGLES

No-trace camping is not no-impact camping. In Goldstream Provincial Park on Vancouver Island, British Columbia, the bald eagle population in the estuary dropped dramatically over several years. When access was closed to all kayaking and hiking in the mouth of the estuary, the eagles returned. Hikers, no matter how silent, and paddlers, no matter how graceful, were driving the eagles away from a food source necessary for their survival.

site: if you packed it in, pack it out, as well as any garbage already there. Leave your campsite better than you found it. There's really no responsible alternative.

473 You need a buffer of at least a hundred yards to minimize your impact on wildlife. In many places in the United States and Canada you are legally required to stay at least that far from all marine mammals. Use your binoculars to get a closer view. You're the visitor, and it's your job to adapt.

474 Be an environmental activist. Record, photograph, and report environmental misuse wherever you paddle.

475 Check with local fish and wildlife authorities before you go touring in new areas. Some areas are denying access to kayaks.

476 Open campfires are seldom necessary. Few will argue against their aesthetics, but many are now considering their effects. Keep campfires small and build them below the tide line. The intertidal zone is more resilient than other biozones.

477 Pick your firewood up off the ground; it's the right size if you can break it with your hands or feet, or use your small saw.

Planning a Day Trip

Each time you go out, even for a short day trip, plan for the unexpected. Bring lots of water, some food, and an emergency shelter. Have the means to stay warm and to get warm if you do get cold. A last-minute decision to go for an brief evening paddle may keep you out overnight. Leave a float plan with someone. Remember, most accidents happen close to home; we spend more time paddling short trips than long expeditions.

Remember to make a plan and carry it out. A good checklist will help you make sure you're prepared to leave. Weather conditions, the paddlers' skills, and your purpose will determine the minimum essentials for a safe and comfortable trip. The items listed here for a day trip would not be sufficient for the most demanding conditions.

Day-Trip Checklist

* Float plan filed with reliable person
* Up-to-date information on weather, tides, winds, waves, swells, and other local hazards
* Compass, charts, tide tables, watch, 360-degree white navigation light
* VHF radio, flares, lights
* Seaworthy and watertight kayak with hatch covers, reserve buoyancy, paddle, sprayskirt
* Paddle float, spare paddle, towline, floating throw line, bilge pump, waterproof flashlight, whistle, horn, helmet
* Personal flotation device (with knife, flares, light stick, strobe)

- Clothing suitable for immersion: wet suit, dry suit, booties, sandals
- Drink on deck, eyeglasses and floating retainer, medications, nutritious lunch and drink

- Clothes for sun, cold, rain, pogies or gloves
- Hat for sun, cold, rain
- Sunscreen, sunglasses
- Kits stored securely and accessibly: first-aid kit, repair kit, bailout pack

Planning a Multiday Trip

Clarify your intentions, goals, and expectations before you go. All trip members must have the same expectations about how far you'll paddle in a day and how fast you'll cover that distance. Plan within the limits of the group. Trips are often intended to stretch limits, but be careful to stretch only one or two. Your capacity for distance, speed, duration, wilderness level, exposure, and solo traveling will be tested sooner or later.

Determine a ratio of paddling to camping. How many days a week will you travel? Will you be breaking camp every day or paddling from a base camp? How many hours will you paddle in one day?

Be clear about how expenses will be shared and keep an account. Make sure everyone carries enough emergency cash.

478 Rule of thirds: A kayaking trip is one-third preparation, one-third execution, and one-third recollection.

479 Each day en route, review your plans. Spend some time in the evening planning for tomorrow. As paddlers gain strength or become tired and as weather systems come and go, adjust the overall plan to make the best of each day.

480 You'll be most comfortable if you paddle in the rain and camp in the sun.

481 GO. There are always reasons not to go. You won't be able to plan for

CHOOSING PADDLING PARTNERS

- Paddle short distances together before you go out on a long trip.
- Avoid paddling partners who say, "I've never capsized."
- Never paddle with anyone who says, "I'll never capsize."
- A good sense of humor will help you move through most difficulties.
- Are they early risers, or do they sleep in till ten?
- How long does it take them to break camp and get under way?
- Do you have complementary kitchen skills? I cook, you clean?
- Do they have the safety equipment and skills needed to rescue you?
- Do they like to spend most of the day hiking along the beach or paddling offshore?
- Are they able to compromise and to alter plans as conditions change?
- Is their general health good? Consider short-term afflictions like the flu and long-term medical conditions. Are they apt to overreact to minor illness and injury?
- Can their level of general fitness (strength and endurance) sustain minimum expectations?
- If they say they can roll their kayaks, don't assume they can roll them in sea conditions rough enough to require a roll.

everything. If it's an interesting trip well worth taking, you'll have to be resilient and creative to complete it.

482 Remain determined but flexible. If bad weather, illness, inadequate fitness, or other unanticipated difficulties interfere, you must adjust accordingly. As soon as possible, communicate any change of plans to the person holding your float plan.

483 Keep a navigation log and a journal. Knowing your speed made good against the wind yesterday will improve your navigation for tomorrow. Make note of good campsites and beaches for landing in a swell and mark them on charts for later reference.

Considerations for Leaders

During simple daylong trips a leader is seldom assigned or chosen, but informally the opinions of the most experienced paddler in the group are often given special consideration. On more technically demanding trips and longer trips there's more need for a clearly identified leader. Regardless of the rigor of the trip or how you choose a leader, several fundamental leadership issues must always be addressed.

Who. Know the limits and expectations of all members of the group.

What. All paddlers must pack necessary equipment; check that it's adequate for needs both on water and on land.

Where. Clarify departure and return locations. List campsites and include alternatives. Know the local weather conditions and tide patterns and how they are affected by geography.

When. Consider the time of year and the tidal cycle. Have a clear understanding of your departure and return dates. Decide when you'll get up each day and how long the group will spend traveling.

Why. Each trip should have a theme or purpose. Research the area; any additional knowledge will enhance your pleasure and safety.

484 If paddling partners can't agree to some simple safety and courtesy rules, paddle with someone else. They're likely to get themselves in trouble and draw you into a risky rescue scenario.

485 Take a wilderness first-aid course. Even day trips can take paddlers where emergency medical treatment may be hours away.

486 Plan for the unexpected. On your float plan include bad-weather escape options, alternative means of communication, and contingency routes to a road and a phone.

487 Clarify the destination and duration of side trips. If members of the group are heading off on their own they should make it clear where they're going, when they'll be back, and at what time you should leave camp and go looking for them.

488 Be attentive to wind direction. There may be daily changes in land and ocean winds, with strong winds regularly occurring at one time of day. Any change in the normal daily cycle is likely to mean a change in the weather and perhaps an approaching storm.

489 Check in with local people. In wilderness areas leave your name and destination with residents, the harbor master, or the general store clerk. If you get stranded, rescuers will be able to narrow down the search area.

490 Before traveling in a new area, research the local weather and tidal patterns. Get local information from someone who has been recommended as reliable, experienced, and well informed. Research daily patterns and find out the most likely early indicators of incoming storms. Anecdotal information may be inaccurate.

491 Be cautious when judging sea conditions by looking downwind. Wind waves break on the downwind side where you can't see it happen. If you decide to leave a sheltered beach with an offshore wind, be very conservative. Sea conditions will be more severe than they look from shore.

492 Be cautious when judging sea conditions by looking upcurrent. Standing waves generated by moving water in a tidal current break upcurrent.

493 Scan the distance for boomers—large waves that break over submerged rocks on a shallow coast. Keep one eye and one ear to seaward at all times; that's where the waves are coming from. Though it may not look appreciably larger, a swell only three feet higher can easily break six feet over your head when it rises over a rock.

494 Record your dead reckoning data. Regularly logging time and distance will let you calculate your speed and reveal information about inshore conditions not generally available on charts. Kayak navigation along the shore can take advantage of otherwise hard to detect back eddies and countercurrents. Arriving well ahead of time may reveal uncharted currents.

495 A group's paddling speed decreases with its size. A good estimate is 3.2 knots minus 0.1 knot for each member of the group. A group of two

This boomer off Brooks Peninsula, B.C., appeared about every ten minutes when the wave size and direction was just right.

travels at approximately 3 knots, and a group of six will slow progress down to 2.6 knots.

496 Charts can be waterproofed with liquid map sealant, or you can brush two very light coats of Thompson's Water Seal onto both sides. Once treated, the chart is water resistant and will stand up to moisture leaking into the chart case or to rain at the campsite.

497 Heavy-duty clear zip-closure bags in the 16-by-24-inch size make good chart cases. They aren't 100 percent waterproof, but they perform well. Put a little tape over the zipper channel to help keep the drips out. You might have to trim a little off the margins of your charts.

498 Make color copies of the chart sections you need for your trip and have them laminated. They'll fit onto your deck and don't require a chart case. If you copy them two-sided you can cover twice the area; if you leave the backs blank you can use the space for notes.

499 On shore you can use a waterproof marking pen to write notes right on the chart. Erase the writing with alcohol or solvent.

500 Indicate the safe route. As a leader, show your fellow paddlers the best way to go. When communication is difficult, followers will go where you point them. If you show them a whirlpool, they might paddle straight for it! Point to the safe route, not at the hazard.

501 When you go ashore, always tie up your kayak, even when it seems unnecessary. A kayak perched on top of a driftwood log is safe only until the log is refloated. A passing ship may send one wave running just high enough up the beach to reach your kayak.

BE A GRACIOUS VISITOR

Approaching a remote village, I knew there was a small restaurant nestled among the boathouses next to the general store. After a week of paddling and eating my own cooking, the thought of a prepared meal was exhilarating. Arriving at the dock, I changed out of my wet paddling gear and put on clean shore clothes. The restaurant overlooked the harbor; it had hardwood floors and tidy tablecloths highlighted by fresh flowers. I sat down, and almost immediately someone brought me a cup of hot coffee. After taking my order, the waitress said she was surprised to see me come into the restaurant. She said kayakers seldom if ever came in, and when they did they tended to drip all over the floor. She felt that sea kayakers stopped only to urinate on the beach and drop off their garbage on the dock.

502 Be a considerate visitor when touring in remote areas.

In small villages drop a dollar, not your garbage, and get to know a little about the community; it will enrich your trip. Present yourself as a courteous and appreciative guest, and people will offer a great deal of help. If you need a rescue or a water taxi or local

When entering a coastal village, it's good manners to go ashore and stop in at the local businesses.

weather and tide information, it will be these local residents who come to your aid.

503 If you're given a lift, always offer to pay for gas.

504 Listen to the sounds of nature. One of the pleasures of touring is hearing natural noises.

505 Plan quiet times, maybe a whole twenty-four hours, and minimize unnecessary conversation. You may need this to help you stop the incessant chatter of the workplace and start to listen for the more subtle sounds around you.

506 Medications have side effects that may be inconsequential at home but are important when you're paddling or camping. Use no-drowsiness antihistamines. Painkillers may mask an injury that should be rested. Alcohol may add to the social pleasure of a meal or a sunset, but misuse might lead to risky behavior far from emergency help. Consequences multiply when help is distant.

Multiday Trip Checklist

- Make a route plan and schedule— determine the total distance you plan to travel and the distance you need to paddle each day.
- Understand the prevailing seasonal weather and sea conditions.
- Make evacuation plans for sickness, injury, or bad weather.
- Make contingency plans that include alternative routes and camping sites.
- Research campsite availability, accessibility, permissions needed, reservations, and fees.

- How many paddlers are in the group?
- Have everyone carry some emergency money.
- Duplicate equipment between paddlers.
- Prepare and practice rescue procedures for towing, reentry, first aid, signals, and communication.
- Choose a trip leader who is experienced and reliable.
- Assign an assistant trip leader to take over in case of malady, mutiny, or mayhem.
- Take along someone who has first-aid qualifications.
- Determine the physical fitness and general health needed to complete the trip. Relate the physical requirements to the remoteness of the area and the need for independence the trip demands.
- Determine the skill level required. Relate the need for technical skill to the demands of the trip.
- Have phone numbers for fisheries, coast guard, weather information, and other contacts.
- Have a list of family and significant others at home or on shore who can act as a support team or who may require support to cope with your absence.
- Establish times to monitor the radio, to phone home, or to leave messages.
- Have a reliable, fully fueled vehicle to get to and from the launching or landing site.
- Have a sturdy and safe roof rack with good tie-downs.

- Arrange for travel to the launch site, directions, and accommodations.
- Confirm ferry schedules, plane routes, and customs clearance.
- Arrange for secure parking. Determine parking fees.
- Confirm that all kayaks are seaworthy and that they have conspicuous colors and reflective tape.
- Be sure hatches and bulkheads are sturdy and watertight.
- Confirm that adequate buoyancy is available if the kayak is fully flooded with one or more hatches open. Store gear in dry bags and use airbags or a sea sock to fill any large vacant space.
- Make sure rudder and skeg control lines are in good operating condition.
- Have a comfortable seat and backrest.
- Precheck deck rigging: deck lines, deck straps, bow line, fixed compass, deck storage, bags, bungees, straps, bilge pump (foot-operated or electric), hatch covers.
- Have a supplementary hand pump.
- Check your bow line attachment.

Packing It All In

The appendix lists "three hundred things to take along" (see page 118–21). Where will you put them? If you're going out for two or three nights you can be extravagant. You'll still need all your paddling, safety, and camping gear, but provisions will take up a modest amount of space, leaving room for luxuries. Fruits and vegetables will keep without special care.

Trips of four days or more place obvious demands on the storage space of most sea kayaks. You'll need to pack carefully and leave behind all but the most desirable luxury items. Perishable foods will deteriorate if not cared for. You can carry all your water on board and won't need to refill containers. With proper planning, you can have an almost unlimited menu throughout the trip.

On trips of four to ten days the well-prepared sea kayaker can travel self-contained, though you'll need to stock up on fresh water after four or five days. Well-chosen perishable foods kept cool and dry will last almost until the last day. If you do run out of bread and salad you won't mind some canned goods or rice and refried beans on the last day.

Trips lasting more than ten days enter the realm of the expedition. Choose goods and provisions with serious consideration for size, weight, and durability. If you can't restock perishables, you'll be eating rehydrated meals and you'll need to replenish your fresh water regularly.

There's one very effective alternative to packing it all in: use your credit card. Gliding up to the beachfront of a seaside lodge and restaurant has a certain appeal. It's not hard to find the motivation to paddle a full day upwind in the rain if your destination promises a hot shower.

A fully loaded sea kayak can easily carry over 100 pounds of gear. The amount of food and equipment an experienced touring sea kayaker can cram into a tiny craft is sometimes beyond belief. The art of packing and unpacking is mastered by intimate participation and a healthy discarding of things that don't work. The kayak is never packed perfectly, and the gear you take is never ideal. Striving for the perfect package is an ongoing adventure that will keep you scanning the outdoor stores and catalogs for years.

507 A sea kayak can be considered to have five stowage areas: the bow, the forward compartment, the cockpit, the aft compartment, and the stern. Although the bow and stern are within the watertight compartments, their narrow shape and small volume make them a special problem when packing.

508 Kayaks with watertight day hatches immediately behind the cockpit offer additional possibilities. This space is close to the center of the kayak and is well suited for heavier items. Things you need while paddling, like cameras, lunches, and dry tops, can be kept on top of the heavier items stored below.

Whatever the tenor of your trip, the fundamentals of packing your kayak are the same. (See illustrations, page 115.)

509 Create a comprehensive, accurate checklist. On the trip, write down items you're missing and items you should have left behind. When you get home, update your checklist for the next time.

510 Test pack your kayak at home.

511 Keep your deck load to a minimum. Items on the back deck increase windage and weathercocking. Anything on deck risks being swept away, getting wet, and interfering with reentry or rolling.

512 Last in, first out. Items that should be loaded last and remain easily accessible are first-aid kit, lunch, tarp, and a change of clothes. If you come ashore in the rain, set up the tarp, change your clothes, bandage your blisters, and have something to eat. Now you can do the rest of the unloading and set up your camp.

513 Balance your load. Where you load the weight in the kayak makes a difference to the performance and hence the safety of the kayak. Ends should remain light for buoyancy and easy turning.

514 Heavy items should be stored low to maximize stability and near the center of the kayak's length to minimize the effort of steering.

515 Lightweight items should be stored in the ends and on top of heavy ones.

516 The bottom is cool, suitable for perishables.

517 Pack a SHOT bag (Second Half of Trip). You can include clean socks, underwear, chocolate, fresh coffee, a clean T-shirt, half your dry pasta, half your food bars, soap, a book of puzzles, and any other rationed items. It will help spread the treats over the full trip. The SHOT bag can be stuffed in a less accessible area and won't have to be unpacked daily. If necessary, you can remove it and immediately hang it in a tree.

518 Pack an EOT bag (End of Trip). Lock the EOT bag in the trunk of the pickup vehicle. Once again everyone will appreciate clean clothes, candy, fresh coffee, or other delicacies. Don't leave anything visible or valuable in your vehicle.

519 A spinnaker sail bag has a large volume and a wide opening that's easy to pack. It will stuff down to almost nothing when not in use and save a lot of work carrying goods over large tidal flats.

How to pack a sea kayak for a multiday voyage.

Items near the forward hatch can be reached easily on or off the water: first-aid kit, lunch, extra clothing.

Inside the cockpit there is room for a hand pump, radio, tow-lines, drinks, snacks, a camera, and often much more. Keep items well secured.

Heaviest items: water and canned goods, pots, and stove.

food

tent

Long, narrow items fit into the stern.

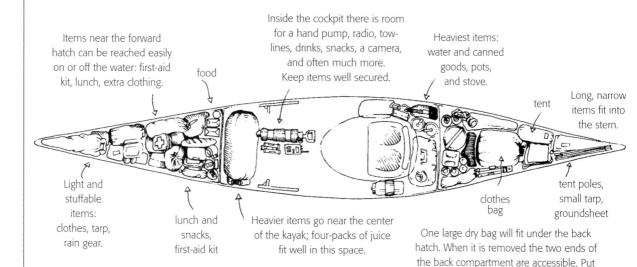

Light and stuffable items: clothes, tarp, rain gear.

lunch and snacks, first-aid kit

Heavier items go near the center of the kayak; four-packs of juice fit well in this space.

clothes bag

tent poles, small tarp, groundsheet

One large dry bag will fit under the back hatch. When it is removed the two ends of the back compartment are accessible. Put kitchen goods, hardware, and repair kit in one end and camp material in the other.

Keep magnetic items away from wherever the compass is mounted.

Smaller, lighter items can go on top of the larger, heavier items below. Food items like dry pasta are well suited to this area.

A hand bilge pump, VHF radio, and flares can fit under the cockpit deck.

Smaller, lighter items can go on top of the larger, heavier items below.

two-piece spare paddle

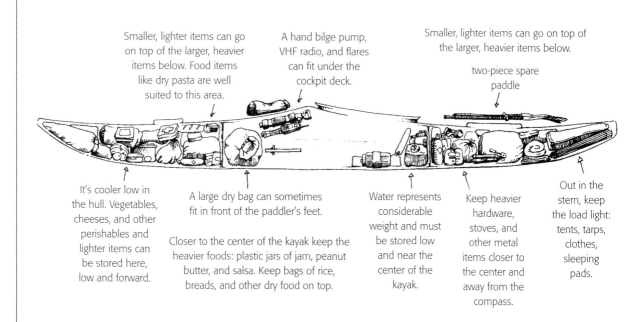

It's cooler low in the hull. Vegetables, cheeses, and other perishables and lighter items can be stored here, low and forward.

A large dry bag can sometimes fit in front of the paddler's feet.

Closer to the center of the kayak keep the heavier foods: plastic jars of jam, peanut butter, and salsa. Keep bags of rice, breads, and other dry food on top.

Water represents considerable weight and must be stored low and near the center of the kayak.

Keep heavier hardware, stoves, and other metal items closer to the center and away from the compass.

Out in the stern, keep the load light: tents, tarps, clothes, sleeping pads.

520 The myriad small bags, kits, containers, and loose items stowed in various places can be dropped into mesh bags and carried up the beach. After you repack your kayak the mesh bags will stuff into a nook ready to be pulled out for the next unpacking.

521 Facial tissues in pocket-sized packages and individually wrapped wet wipes pack well. Keep them with toiletries, in your day pack, and with the first-aid supplies.

522 Unpack your kayak before lifting it. Your back will thank you, your kayak will thank you.

523 Organize your load to help you remember where you put everything, such as always storing the pantry up against the forward bulkhead and camp items, tent, tarp, and sleeping pad in the stern.

524 Use dry bags judiciously to protect your gear and maintain reserve buoyancy in case of a leak.

525 Label each bag with the contents and the owner.

526 Lightweight coated nylon dry bags are less bulky and slide better, but they're not always as durable. Rolled closures on some dry bags made of heavier rubberized material add significant volume to the load and don't slide easily into small spaces.

527 Keep sunscreen, bug dope (DEET), and any other oil- or solvent-based products well away from your dry bags. They'll dissolve the coating.

528 Keep dry bags out of the sun. Apply some ultraviolet protectant to the outside of your dry bags.

529 Long, skinny bags are best suited to the spaces inside a kayak. The residual air inside the dry bag can take up valuable space. Though this air adds a margin of safety to a flooded kayak, too much retained air is lost stowage.

Unpacking two kayaks yields, a variety of dry bags and small containers.

530 Where space is at a premium, avoid double bagging, since each bag holds air. Items that can afford to get damp will take up less space if not packed in bags; rain pants, nylon pants, or a fleece sweater will stuff into small spaces that would otherwise be unusable. Smaller loose items can go in those irregular spaces where a dry bag won't fit.

531 When sliding that last large bag into a tight space, stuff the bag into place first, then close its top. This lets the bag conform to fit the space more precisely.

532 Some dry bags come with vents that let air under pressure escape. This can be very helpful in cramming a tapered bag into the bow or stern.

533 Fill pots and pans with items such as cherry tomatoes or a bag of pancake mix. This uses the space and protects the contents.

534 Pack your tent in two or three parts. Separate the poles from the fabric tent and fly. Put the fly cover in one long, thin bag, the tent in another, and the poles in a third. These narrow, pliable bags will pack more efficiently than one large bag.

535 The cockpit space in front of your feet can be quite large. Foot pegs may interfere with the ease of packing, but there's too much space there to neglect. One large heavy-gauge dry bag will fit horizontally, or two medium bags will jam in vertically. This is a good place to use compression straps on a bag. This area can take a good deal of weight since it's near the center of the kayak.

536 **Safety note:** All items stowed in the cockpit must be secured by lash-

WHERE'S MY SPOON?

Circumstance brought two solo sea kayakers together on a tiny islet beach. The experienced paddler sat quietly and watched the novice frantically unpack his kayak and make camp. Bags and boxes would repeatedly come out and go back in. By the time dinner was over, my frenzy for packing and unpacking and looking for my frequently lost spoon must have either amused or irritated my more experienced dinner guest. I settled down after the dishes were clean and my elusive spoon was once more packed away, waiting to be lost and found. Having hardly moved since I first arrived, he calmly told me that after three or four days of traveling I'd be able to slow down and would know where everything was without having to search. He was right. After a few days I could make and break camp in an hour, efficiently picking out the items I needed from the maze of bags and jars. After many years of kayak camping, it still takes me two or three days to get into the rhythm of living out of a kayak, but my little green bag of eating utensils remains the most elusive of all my gear.

ings or other permanent fixtures that will firmly restrain them if you have to make a wet exit in strong surf. This is a stringent requirement. Even if you can afford to lose the items overboard, loose items are likely to interfere with your reentering the cockpit.

537 Look for small spaces beside your seat. Seats hung from the cockpit the vertical seat supports and the hull. There may be room for flares, a rolled-up rain jacket, and tent or tarp poles. Some kayaks may have enough space to store a rolled tarp here.

538 Heavy items or items that you need soon after arriving on shore can go behind your seat. Although it may seem like a good place for items you need while paddling, this space can be blocked by folding seat backs and hard to reach.

Three Hundred Things to Take Along

For trips of more than one day, this list tries to cover all the items you must take, should take, and might consider taking. Your paddling environment and the duration of your trip will dictate what is a necessity and what might be a luxury. For fall paddling in the Queen Charlotte Islands, items to keep you warm and dry might take precedence over carrying drinking water, whereas in Baja California water would be more important.

Basic Paddling Gear

personal flotation device (PFD)
paddling jackets (2)
dry suit, wet suit for cool or cold water
footwear for paddling—booties, mukluks, sandals
sprayskirts (2)
paddle
paddle leash
spare paddle
paddle float

Personal Dry Bag

wallet and keys (might be stored in clothes bag for safety)
eyeglasses (two pairs)
sunglasses
toilet paper
sunscreen (lots)
lip balm (SPF rated)
camera and film
medications

In Your PFD

light stick
rocket flares
smoke flares
whistle
folding knife
towline

Cockpit Accessible

heaving line
water—1 quart minimum (or electrolyte replacement drink)
sponge
helmet

Traveling Snacks

24-ounce bottles of water, fruit juice, or sports drink
bananas
crackers (cheese, peanut butter)
bagels (spread with cream cheese, marmalade)
energy bars
carrots, green beans, apples, pears
prepared sandwiches
nuts and dried fruit
thermos (with a hot beverage or soup)
candy, chocolate

Navigation Gear

diver's slate (on deck)
watch (on deck)
deck compass
hand-bearing or hiker's compass
nautical charts or maps (1:40,000), waterproof map case(s)
guidebook
parallel ruler, marking pen
tide tables, pilot instructions

waterproof logbook and
  pencil
headlamp
strobe light
waterproof flashlight
spare batteries
spare bulbs
360-degree white navigation
  light
global positioning system
  (GPS)

Safety Equipment

whistle
air horn
bivvy sack, survival bag
spare rope, bungee cord
knife
signal mirror
distress signals
light stick
aerial flares
handheld flares
smoke canisters
drogue (sea anchor)
emergency food bars
VHF radio, mobile phone
EPIRB (emergency position
  indicating radio beacon)

Hardware

binoculars
waterproof transistor radio
spare batteries
flashlight
flashlight bulbs
light sticks
candles
matches/lighter
fire starter fuel
pliers, screwdrivers
screws
multitool

diver's knife
machete, ax, camp saw
needle and thread
seam sealant
no-see-um netting
extra tent pole sleeve and
  ferrule
stainless steel hooks or carabiners
flexible wire
duct tape, masking tape,
  electrician's tape
five-minute epoxy glue
whipping twine
aluminum foil (heavy-duty)
orange plastic survival bags
⅛-inch plywood the size of
  hatch cover

First-Aid Kit

painkillers (aspirin/ibupro-
  fen/acetaminophen/para-
  cetamol/Tylenol with
  codeine)
chemical heat packs (Heat
  Wave provides 110°F for
  six to ten hours)
chemical cold pack
seasickness pills or patches
antidiarrhea medication
  (Pepto-Bismol tablets)
antacid tablets (Tums)
laxative
antihistamine (Benadryl)
no-drowsiness decongestant
topical antibiotic (Poly-
  sporin, Bactroban)
butterfly bandages
pressure bandage
4-inch-square gauze pads
2-inch-square nonstick pads
triangular bandage
waterproof bandages

cotton adhesive tape
adhesive-backed nylon tape
  (Spenco)
safety pins
fine-tipped tweezers (for
  slivers)
sterile needles (for slivers)
vinegar (for sea stingers)
cotton balls
cotton swabs
eyedrops
topical oral anesthetic
rectal thermometer
tongue depressor
petroleum jelly
moleskin
Mylar survival blanket

Bailout Pack

compass
light stick
flares
signal mirror
whistle
emergency food bars
orange plastic survival
  bag
candles
flashlight
matches/lighter
wax fire starters
first-aid kit
fishing tackle
identification
knife
Mylar survival blanket

Clothing

wet footwear—neoprene
  booties, kayaking or river
  shoes
dry footwear—sandals,
  shoes, boots, sneakers,

walking shoes, or hiking
    boots
gloves—cutoff gloves, neo-
    prene gloves, pogies
headgear—shade hat, rain
    hat, warm hat
sun gear—sunglasses, sun-
    screen, long-sleeved shirt
cold wear—thermal quick-
    dry socks, leggings, pants,
    undershirt, vest, hat,
    watch cap
warm wear—shorts, long-
    sleeved light shirt, sun hat
wet wear—rain jacket and
    pants
spare clothes
undershirts (2)
sun jacket, shirt
sou'wester

Toiletries
toothbrush, toothpaste,
    dental floss
soap, shampoo, deodorant
towel
nailbrush
nail clippers
nail file
toilet paper
hairbrush, comb
facial tissue
cotton swabs
biodegradable liquid
    camp soap (one kind
    for everyone—and all
    uses)
lip balm (SPF rated)
sunscreen

Camping Equipment
tent
insect repellent

flashlight(s), candle lantern
    (separate from safety
    lights)
clock
pillow
pieces of light rope
tarpaulin
inflatable sleeping pad
    (Therm-a-Rest)
sleeping bag
sleeping bag liner
groundsheet
day pack, fanny pack
foldable frameless backpack
shovel
mesh bags (2)

Kitchen Equipment
stove
fuel bottle
fire starters
waterproof matches in
    sealed container
bowl, plate, cup
knife, fork, spoon
kitchen spoons
can opener
pots and pans
candle lantern (with extra
    candles)
garbage bags
dishcloth
pot scrubber
dish towel

Groceries
3 to 4 quarts of water per
    person per day
hot chocolate mix
tea, herbal tea
coffee
iced tea mix (also as hot
    drink)

sugar
4- or 6-packs of ultrapas-
    teurized milk, powdered
    milk
4- or 6-packs juice (quarts)
foil packs of dried soup
    (1-cup size)
bouillon cubes
granola, cereal
rice, pasta, noodles
couscous
dry tortellini
whole wheat buns
dry biscuits
pita bread, bagels, bread-
    cheese sticks
crackers, English muffins
tortillas
biscuit mix, pancake mix
salt, pepper, curry powder,
    herbs, spices
soy sauce, chili powder or
    paste
olive oil
eggs (fresh, hard-boiled,
    pickled)
grated Parmesan
cheese (small, vacuum-
    sealed)
peanut butter
baked beans
dehydrated refried beans,
    black beans, bulgur
    wheat
fresh or dried tomatoes,
    mushrooms, sauerkraut
small potatoes
onions, garlic, chives, shal-
    lots
zucchini, greens, carrots,
    cabbage, cherry tomatoes,
    green beans, carrots
canned corn (small)

vacuum-sealed hard
    salami, pepperoni,
    etc.
canned meats (tuna,
    chicken, sardines or
    kippers)
cans of stew
cans of chowder
canned olives, tomatoes,
    water chestnuts
squeezable margarine

relish, mayonnaise, mustard
    (foil packs)
fruit salad
dried fruit, banana chips
salted nuts
jam, marmalade
candy, mints

Entertainment
swimming gear, face mask,
    snorkel

waterproof camera, camera
    leash, film
reading and writing materials
fishing gear—rod, reel, line,
    lures, gill line, dip net
fishing license and local regu-
    lations
cards, games

Lines and Knots

Boats and rope go hand in hand. A little skill with rope will alleviate much frustration and help keep your kayak safely on your roof rack. Tents and tarps depend on ropes and knots. Modern rope is highly engineered and made of a wide variety of fibers in several forms. Braided line is the best for use around small boats; braided outer and inner layers make it strong and flexible. Polyester line is preferred for most uses because it resists ultraviolet light and won't rot. It stretches little when wet or under load, so your deck lines will stay the way they were tied. On the roof rack your tie-down lines stay taut and keep your expensive boat snug.

Rolling Hitch
A rolling hitch is used to secure one line to another line when the strain is near to parallel. It also works well to tie off an adjustable line for a tarp, tent, or

clothesline. To tie one, wrap the working end twice around the standing part and tie a half hitch above the knot to dispose of the end (1). Before finishing the knot, it is important to jam the second wrap behind the first (2).

Run the line from the corner of the tarp out and around a

branch or tent peg. Tie a rolling hitch back onto the returning end of the line. You can pull the knot up the line and snug it into place and it won't slack off. When it's time to take the tarp down, grasp the entire knot and slide it loose. It will move easily when pushed but won't move when pulled.

Rolling hitch.

Rolling hitch in use.

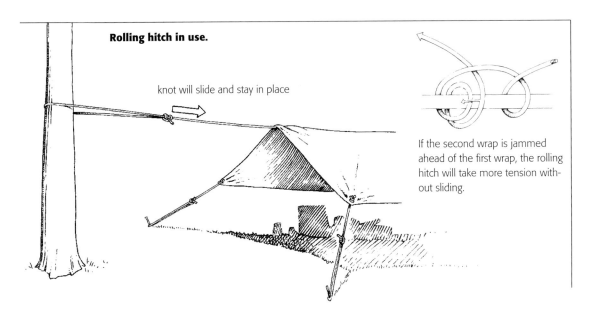

knot will slide and stay in place

If the second wrap is jammed ahead of the first wrap, the rolling hitch will take more tension without sliding.

Lark's Head Knot

A lark's head is useful in many situations, especially when a knot will have a strain near 90 degrees.

If a second wrap is formed, the lark's head becomes a prusik knot.

Prusik Knot

Much like a rolling hitch, a prusik will take strain when pulled but will slide easily when pushed. To tie a prusik you need a loop of line. Tie a simple lark's head knot, add a second

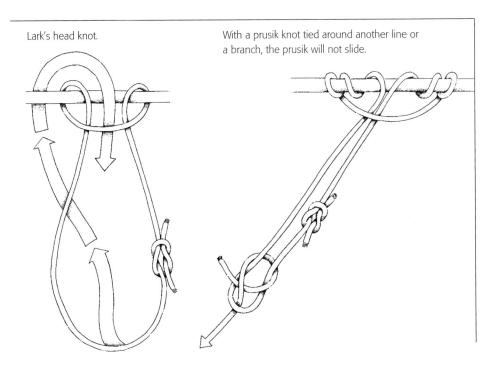

Lark's head knot.

With a prusik knot tied around another line or a branch, the prusik will not slide.

wrap around the standing line, and you have a prusik. Pull the knot up snug; if pulled on the knot will stay in place and take considerable load. When pushed it will slide easily. When trees don't co-operate and the angle of your tarp guy-line needs adjusting, a prusik can help you out.

Trucker's Hitch

A trucker's hitch is used to tie down a load securely. If the first loop is tied correctly it will also undo easily and leave you a line free of knots. A trucker's hitch is commonly used to tie a kayak to a roof rack. It can also be used in place of a rolling hitch for tent and tarp guylines.

To tie a trucker's hitch, first form a loop with a bight of line. The loop must be formed with the running end (1). Next pass the running end around the roof rack, tree, or other object, and back through and bent over the loop. When the line is pulled tight (2), dispose of the end with one or two half hitches tied close to the loop (3).

A Quick-Tie Bowline

If you know only one knot, the bow-line is a good choice. Most Scouts, Guides, Rangers, and Beavers learn this knot with the time-honored mnemonic

A bowline.

about the rabbit going around the tree and through the hole. This is generally the same technique used for the sailor's one-handed bowline. Both of these techniques work well when the line is running away from you, and the knot is tied with the loop toward you. Count-less times I've watched someone strug-gle to tie a bowline onto a kayak or a

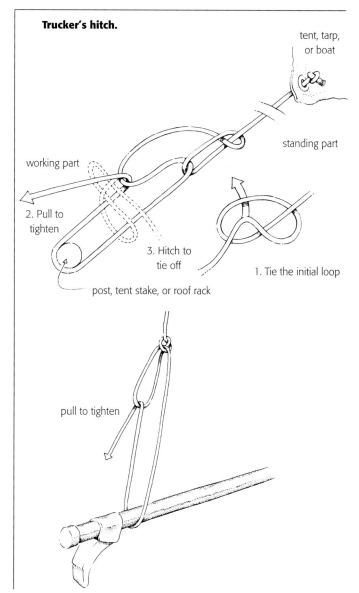

Trucker's hitch.

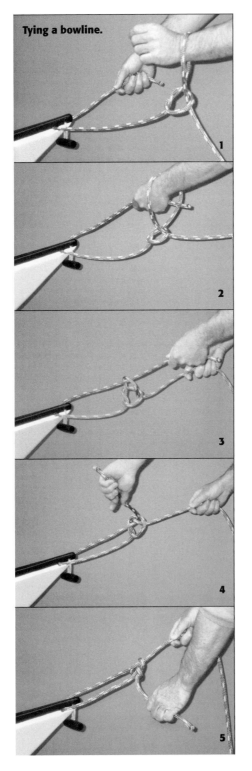

Tying a bowline.

sail, reciting the rabbit-and-tree story or attempting the "twist of the wrist" move that sailors use, but unable to easily tie the knot. More often than not the problem is that the bowline needs to be tied looping away from you, as when a rescuer tries to tie a bowline onto another kayak.

First pretie a running loop in the standing part of the line; keep the knot open and loose with your hand within the running loop. With a little practice you can do this with a twist of your hand (1). With the end of the line in the other hand, pass the line out and around whatever the bowline is to be fastened to, such as a bouncing kayak or your hard-to-reach roof rack (2). Next, give the end of the line to the hand that's within the loop (3). (Note that you need access to the object for only a split second.) Once the loop of line has passed around the object you can retire to tie the knot quite separately. Draw your hand out of the loop, still keeping the running loop and knot open and loose (4). With your free hand, grasp the standing part below the knot. Now here's the trick: fold the line back on itself and pull on the standing part (5). Bam! You've got a bowline.

Practice with a piece of ⅜-inch braided line and a fixed object like a fence rail or a branch. Before long you'll master the quick-tie bowline.

Figure-Eight Stopper Knot

The figure-eight stopper knot is a simple stopper knot used on the end of a line.

Clove Hitch

The clove hitch is one of those don't-leave-home-without-it knots. It

A clove hitch.

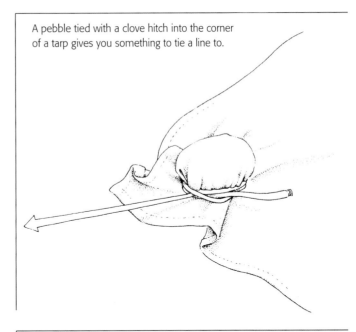

A pebble tied with a clove hitch into the corner of a tarp gives you something to tie a line to.

can be used almost anywhere you have to tie off the end of a line.

The clove hitch can be tied two ways. For fitting over a post, log, or branch, first tie two overhand loops. Lay the first loop over the second to form the clove hitch and place the fully formed knot over the end of the post.

The other way to tie a clove hitch is to pass the end of a line twice around an object. On the first pass, lay the line over the standing part, and on the second pass, slip it under the standing part.

Spiral Hitching

Spiral hitching is useful wherever you might use common whipping and for many more demanding applications. It's simply a set of repeated hitches. The advantage of hitching over whipping is that each wrap of the twine is knotted and secure from unraveling. The two ends of a deck bungee can be spiral hitched, as can the ends of deck lines. Hitching in this case avoids bulky knots. Bound tightly, the ends of your bungees or deck lines will not work themselves free. Melting or gluing the ends and covering the hitching with a few wraps of black electrician's tape finishes the job off nicely. Loops of line can be lashed onto perimeter deck lines with

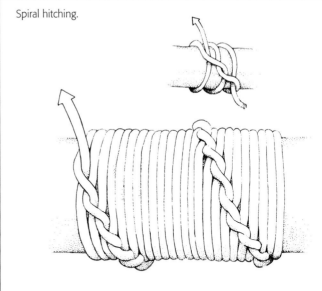

Spiral hitching.

spiral hitching to create points for towing or other attachments.

Sheet Bend

The sheet bend is simple and useful. It holds well when under a steady strain and is easy to undo. Tie the working end to a bight of line or a loop and pass it through the loop, around the standing part, and underneath itself.

Quick-Release or Slippery Sheet Bend

You can create a quick-release knot by looping the line under the knot rather than feeding the end straight through it. Always leave the end of the line knot-free so that when the sheet bend is released, the bitter end can pass through the loop without becoming caught.

Daisy-Chaining

A daisy chain is useful for shortening a towline. You can shorten a line to one-third its original length by tying a series of slip knots. To prevent the last link from unraveling, attach a small clip. By adjusting the position of the clip, you can adjust the line length.

The first link . . .

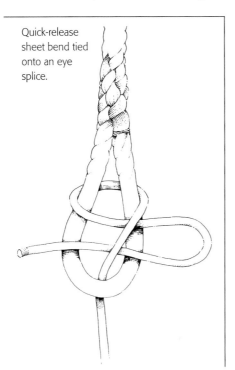

Quick-release sheet bend tied onto an eye splice.

. . . of a daisy chain.

Glossary

abeam On a bearing or direction at 90 degrees to the centerline of the kayak. Off to the side.

bilge The lowest point of the interior of the hull where water collects.

bracing Paddle strokes that provide support to prevent a capsize. *See* high brace; low brace.

bombproof A paddler is said to have a bombproof roll if her roll is reliable at all times, especially in the most adverse conditions.

broaching When traveling down the face of a wave, the uncontrolled changing of direction from down the wave to across the wave. The result of an uncontrolled broach is often a capsize.

bulkhead Any vertical interior panel, often watertight, that separates one portion of the hull from another. An example is the forward bulkhead that separates the cockpit area from the forward compartment in most sea kayaks.

carabiner A large, palm-size clip that opens and closes by means of a spring-loaded gate. Many carabiners are specifically designed for technical rock climbing equipment.

catenary cut A technique of cutting and sewing fabric to form a rain- and wind-shedding curve when strung between two or more points.

coaming Pieces projecting above the deck that meet the sprayskirt, forming a seal to keep water out of the cockpit.

combat roll A successful Eskimo roll after capsizing unexpectedly in adverse conditions.

control side On a feathered paddle, the side of the paddle on which the paddle blade is in a natural position and the hand retains a firm grip at all times.

edge control The ability to maintain the kayak on an angle with one hull or deck seam underwater. Increases the maneuverability of the kayak.

fairlead A fitting or structure used to keep a line running straight and true—without kinks or bends.

feathered blades Paddle blades positioned at different angles to each other.

fingerboard A short (8 inches) rubber or plastic supplemental attachment on a round paddle shaft. Permits the paddler, by sense of touch, to determine the orientation of the paddle blades.

flotation bags Air-filled bags placed in the kayak to maintain buoyancy in the event of a leak or capsize.

foot brace Pedal-like foot rest, often adjustable. Provides greater maneuvering control.

gate hook A spring-loaded opening on a carabiner or other snap hook that opens by pivoting around a hinge point.

high brace A supportive bracing stroke where the paddler's hands are higher than the elbows and the power face of the paddle is braced against the surface of the water.

low brace A supportive bracing stroke where the paddler's hands are lower than the elbows and the back face of the paddle is braced against the surface of the water.

lubber line A line or point on the bowl of a marine compass that is aligned to view the bow of the kayak along the longitudinal centerline of the kayak and the pivot point of the swinging plate of the compass.

maytagged Capsizing in a turbulent wave; often has a washing-machine like effect.

offside The noncontrol side when using a feathered paddle. This is the left side for a paddler using a right-hand-control paddle and the right side for a paddler using a left-hand-control paddle.

paddle float A buoyant rigid or inflatable float fastened to one paddle blade. Helps provide support when reentering a kayak in deep water.

pearling Capsizing a kayak end-for-end while surfing down the face of a wave.

PFD (personal flotation device) A vest or jacket specifically designed to provide sufficient buoyancy for a person in the water to stay afloat. Coast guard regulations require one coast guard–approved PFD per person on a boat.

pogies A mitten-like glove usually made of neoprene or nylon that fits around the paddle shaft.

puck-style compass A marine hand-bearing compass that is flat and circular and fits in the user's palm.

sculling A stroke where the paddle is passed back and forth over the surface of the water in a repeated arcing motion. Supports the paddler and kayak in a partial capsize.

sea sock A flexible waterproof fabric liner/bag that forms a hull liner large enough to accommodate a seated paddler when firmly attached to the cockpit coaming and placed inside the cockpit. It is used in kayaks without integral watertight compartments and will prevent excessive water from entering the hull.

setup The posture and paddle position taken prior to an Eskimo roll.

sheer line The uppermost line in a profile view of the kayak's hull.

skeg A short length of keel in the stern area of the kayak. Often an adjustable, vertically pivoting fin that, when lowered, alters the weathercocking and tracking of the kayak.

sprayskirt Usually made of neoprene or nylon. Fits around the paddler's waist and fastens around the cockpit and prevents water from entering the cockpit.

strumbox A fitting placed on the inlet end of a pump hose and secured to the hull. Increases the efficiency of the pump by reducing the turbulence of the water entering the hose.

sweep A turning paddle stroke that usually starts close to the kayak and sweeps outward away from the kayak.

toggle A short handle attached by a line to the kayak. End toggles are located at the extreme ends of the kayak. They hang free so they can be grasped by a swimmer during a kayak rescue. Lifting toggles, positioned on the deck near the ends, are for carrying the kayak when on shore.

weathercocking The tendency of a kayak to turn independently in an upwind direction. Most common when your course is perpendicular to the wind's direction.

windage The area of the kayak above the waterline, in profile.

Metric Conversion Table

1 inch	2.54 centimeters	1 quart	0.946 liters
1 inch	25.4 millimeters	1 knot	1.85 kilometers/hour
1 foot	0.3 meters	1 mile/hour	1.609 kilometers/hour
1 ounce	28.35 grams	1 nautical mile	1.85 kilometers
1 pound	0.45 kilograms	°F	°C × 1.8 + 32
1 fluid ounce	29.573 milliliters	°C	(°F − 32) × 0.555